C000156327

"This book takes an insight of Cardinal Luis Tagle, one dynamic Catholic leaders ai church's horizon. It is a con rich biographical detail and thought-provoking personal reflections. In Tagle's vision, the modern church must engage people through humility, simplicity, and, as the book's subtitle states, 'learning by listening.'"

—John Thavis
Author of New York Times best-seller, *The Vatican Diaries*

"As head of the Rome Bureau of the world's premiere English Catholic News Service, Cindy Wooden has written a brilliant biography of one of the great lights of the Post-Conciliar Church. Cardinal Tagle has said: 'A person will always be deeper than any label. And no person, especially when talking about deep mysteries of love, marriage, relationships, can ever be labeled.' But when you finish reading Wooden's story of Chito, you cannot help but label him 'good.' Cardinal Luis Antonio Tagle is a shepherd who not only has the smell of the sheep and the mind and heart of the Good Shepherd but the manner and courage of the Bishop of Rome. Francis and Chito are cut from the same cloth. Of all the WITNESS interviews I have ever done for our TV network, the moments with Cardinal Chito were among the most powerful and beautiful."

—Fr. Thomas Rosica, CSB
CEO, Salt + Light Catholic Media Foundation, Canada
English Language Attaché, Holy See Press Office

Luis Antonio Tagle

Leading by Listening

Cindy Wooden

LITURGICAL PRESS
Collegeville, Minnesota

www.litpress.org

Cover design by Stefan Killen Design. Cover illustration by Philip Bannister.

1   2   3   4   5   6   7   8   9

Library of Congress Control Number: 2015936997

ISBN 978-0-8146-3717-3   978-0-8146-3742-5 (ebook)

Contents

Acknowledgments

I would like to thank Cardinal Luis Antonio Tagle who, although initially reluctant to see a biography of himself published, generously spent hours answering my questions. In addition to being essential for writing this short biography, spending time with the cardinal was thought provoking and a real blessing. I'd also like to thank his staff for making me feel so welcome and looking after me in Manila.

Father Joseph Komonchak and Jesuit Fr. Daniel Huang also put up with my questions, answered them, and provided direction for other areas to explore.

I thank my colleagues at Catholic News Service, especially Anthony J. Spence, director and editor in chief, for their support of this undertaking. John Thavis, author and the former CNS Rome bureau chief, provided encouragement and made great suggestions for improving the text. Thanks to Barry Hudock, J. Andrew Edwards, and the other folks at Liturgical Press who exercised extreme patience while I completed the manuscript. And I thank the Franciscan Friars of the Atonement for allowing me to access Centro Pro Unione, their wonderful library in Rome.

In addition to interviews with the cardinal, I attended so many speeches he gave in Rome over the course of two years that he may have thought I was stalking him. But I also have cited comments Cardinal Tagle made in a wide-ranging interview with Basilian Fr. Thomas Rosica of Canada's Salt and Light Television (http://youtu.be/eu4ooS5H8sA).

Further information came from the websites of the Archdiocese of Manila (www.rcam.org), the news site of the Catholic Bishops' Conference of the Philippines (www.cbcpnews.com), the International Eucharistic Congress in Dublin (www.iec2012.ie), and the Vatican website (www.vatican.va) for texts of Cardinal Tagle's speeches at various gatherings of the Synod of Bishops and at the 2008 International Eucharistic Congress in Quebec.

Introduction

Luis Antonio "Chito" Gokim Tagle's road to the red hat was paved by a strong extended family, a solid education, the kindness of strangers, and a priest who tricked him into taking the seminary entrance exam. Seriously. It bothered him so much when he failed that exam, he began daily Eucharistic adoration to discern whether his vocation was as a doctor—as he and his parents had planned—or as a priest.

Much of this book is based on hours of interviews with Cardinal Tagle conducted in February, May, and October 2014 in Rome and in January 2015 in Manila. The interviews followed several conversations over a period of months aimed at convincing the cardinal that his cooperation would not be presented as an attempt on his part to gain attention or, worse, to show off. In fact, he agreed to speak to the author only on the condition that a biography would reflect his belief that anything he has accomplished and anything he has learned about living the Christian life is the result of being loved and taught by special people and listening to the poor.

His nickname, Chito, is a constant reminder of his status in his family and in the world, he said. The nickname is so much part of his identity that it is included in the Italian version of his official biography on the Vatican website's section on the College of Cardinals. It's a diminutive of Luiscito, which in turn is the diminutive of Luis. His mother, Milagros, always called him Chito, but sometimes, he says, his grandmother would call him Luiscito, and that meant trouble because in his house, the long form was never an endearment. The little "ito" suffix on names is common in the Philippines, a land of people known by their nicknames. With its constant use, he said, "you never grow up. You're always the diminutive. It's a reminder that you are a child."

Gokim, which he also insists on using, is his mother's maiden name. The Chinese surname is a strong part of his identity. His maternal grandfather traveled with a relative from China to the Philippines at the age of thirteen, decided to stay, and eventually married. He worked for a cigarette company in the Philippines, traveling often as he brought cigarettes and cigars from Manila to the country's northern districts. "He was not a person of high education," the cardinal said, "but he made sure all of his children—nine of them—went to university. He died a poor, simple person, not owning anything, not owning property, but he had his dreams fulfilled."

The cardinal never met his paternal grandfather, Florencio Tagle, who was a teacher. During the Second World War, a bomb fell near the family's home, but it did not explode. Florencio tried to move it to keep the family safe, but it exploded and killed him immediately, leaving his wife to raise their five children on her own. To support the family, she and her sister opened a *carinderia*, which is a small restaurant. Florencio's son, Manuel—the cardinal's father— was thirteen years old at the time. Eventually his four sisters went to work in the carinderia, and Manuel, the only boy, was the only one of the children to go to university.

At his installation as archbishop of Manila in late 2011, Tagle told the congregation, "As I embark on my new ministry as archbishop of Manila, I feel deeply united with the many beloved disciples who have taught me to recognize the Lord: my loving parents, Manuel and Milagros, and brother Manuel Jr. They have always provided a haven of love and commitment for me; [and] my aunts, uncles, cousins, and clan who never fail to nurture me." He also spoke of each teacher he had from grade school through grad school, the people he worked with on commissions and councils of the Federation of Asian Bishops' Conferences, and the people at the Vatican. And also his "former students, seminarians, the religious and the poor, the beloved poor, who have taught me to be more sensitive to the presence of Jesus who calls me to mission. Your love has enabled me to see the Lord."[1]

Born in Manila on June 21, 1957, Tagle grew up about fifteen miles south of the city in Imus in a house owned by his paternal grandparents and shared with his father's four sisters and their families. The rest of the extended family would gather there for holidays, birthdays, and anniversaries because his grandmother and great-grandmother lived there too.

With fourteen family members in residence, plus two women who helped care for Chito's great-grandmother, the house sounds like a mansion. But Tagle said it was just a regular house. It had one kitchen and one living room where the family would gather. For most of his life, the house also had only one bathroom, which meant that morning schedules were carefully organized and strictly adhered to. As for the bedrooms, Chito and Manuel Jr. slept on the floor of their parents' room. His three unmarried aunts shared a room. His married aunt, her husband, and three children shared another room.

Today a search of YouTube, the internet video site, returns dozens of results with clips of the cardinal singing everything from show tunes to hymns. Music and singing, while perfected and formalized in the seminary, also began at home. One of the women who helped in the house when he was growing up taught Filipino folk songs to him, his brother, and his cousins at a young age. "People saw that I could follow rhythm and music," Tagle said. "If I don't have the time or energy to walk or engage in more physical exercise, if I'm too tired, what relaxes me is music."

The cardinal's parents, both retired bank employees, live today in the same house in Imus. His brother, Manuel Jr., who is five years younger, lives and works in the state of Virginia. A little girl was born to the family a year after Chito was born, but she lived only a few minutes.

Chito already was in school when his little brother was born, and he was in high school when Manuel Jr. was in grade school. Chito entered the seminary as his brother was finishing grade school, "so the time we had living together in the same house wasn't that long," the cardinal said. When Chito went to The Catholic University of America in Washington, DC, for his doctoral studies, Manuel Jr. was working in Chicago, but he and a cousin then moved to Virginia for work and that geographical proximity enabled the brothers to solidify a new relationship as young adults. "And now, since we have our parents to—uh, uh—monitor," he said, smiling at how he found a word that his parents wouldn't find offensive, "we have this common concern. You engage in common discernment and common decision making and that helps in forging a deeper relationship."

After dinner at his parents' house not long ago, he said his mother thanked him and Manuel Jr. for bringing new friends into their lives. She said people know that she and

Manuel Sr. are alone in Imus and offer help and support for them out of admiration for their sons.

Having moved from a family home with sixteen residents directly to the seminary with dozens, living alone was not part of the cardinal's life experience. Even now he lives with two priests and two sisters who manage the residence. He said, "I've never lived in an apartment by myself; I've always lived in community." Growing up in a house shared with so many people "taught us discipline, respect for each other's space and each other's needs. The family experience taught me how to be sensitive to differences and how to handle conflicts at a very early age. Since the people involved were family, you would not allow conflict and differences to lead to divisions; you had to face those conflicts and handle them for a higher good, which is the family."

His family history, both the ethnic mix as well as the strong extended family ties, are very much the Philippine norm. "We assimilate others, and we get assimilated so quickly that sometimes we can be confused. What does it mean to be a Filipino?" he commented. "My mother is half Chinese. My grandfather was born in China, a convert to Christianity, and got married to a Filipino-Chinese woman in the northern part of the Philippines. I don't even understand the language of my mother," a dialect from her home province of Pangasinan. "When she speaks with her brothers and sisters, we're outsiders."

Like many other bishops of Asia who work together in the Federation of Asian Bishops' Conferences, Cardinal Tagle insists the ability to dialogue is a key feature of being a Catholic in Asia where the Christian community is a small minority and where people of different religions, languages, cultures, and ethnicities mix on a daily basis and often intermarry. In Filipino families, he said, "You experience real intercultural dialogue, even interreligious dialogue to some extent. Dialogue must happen in the family, not just in academic circles."

Dealing with differences within the family forces parents to ask serious questions and find solutions that, while affirming the Catholic faith, demonstrate respect for the faith that is a part of the other's identity, he said. Couples of different religions must make decisions about how they will raise their children. "There is a Catholic tradition that is afraid of eclecticism, but if you are a child of a Christian mother and a Hindu father, how do you avoid the eclecticism?" the cardinal asked. "And how do we equip people who will enter into interreligious relationships and family life? Canonically, it's easy: the non-Christian partner signs a document saying, 'I will not hinder the Catholic partner from raising the children. . . .' But in day-to-day life, what will we eat, what practices will we follow, what schools will our children go to, what feasts will we celebrate? Which holidays? How often should the children go to the grandparents who are Hindu? When they visit the Hindu grandparents are they allowed to offer flowers? These are daily concerns that cannot be captured in a few formulae."

Although Cardinal Tagle's Grandfather Gokim was never "a fanatic Buddhist" and converted to Catholicism before he married, throughout his life he maintained some traditional Buddhist practices, including "on certain occasions, offering food and incense to honor the ancestors. He never went back to China; he never saw his mother again or his grandparents. He stayed in the Philippines. So on those once-a-year occasions, he had a photo of his mother and food there and incense."

When the young Chito entered the seminary, his cousins wondered how he would react to his grandfather's ritual and if he would continue to take part. He said he told them, "I know our grandfather, I know he is not committing idolatry here. This is maybe the child in him that wants to express a certain reverence and connection to his mother, who he hadn't seen again since he was thirteen years old. So why wouldn't we join him." The cardinal said that when he was growing up, the ritual was that his grandfather would prepare a plate of food to honor the memory of his mother and would prepare separate plates for his grandchildren. "He was very strict, and would warn the children, 'Don't take any of the food offered for your grandmother or you will get a stomachache.'"

In an interview for this book, the cardinal said his family's history and the living reminders of it, which are on display at every family gathering, keep him from becoming "proud and mighty and lofty."

His family and his connectedness to them are also part of his more academic presentations. At the Asian Mission Congress in 2006, while he was still bishop of Imus, he focused on the importance of stories and the power of personal witness in spreading the Gospel.

> Stories reveal personal identity and people and events that shaped that identity. As I tell my little stories, my fundamental life story is revealed not only to the listener but also and primarily to me, the narrator. I make sense of myself. But I realize in the process that the story is not simply about me. It is also always about other people, my family and friends, society, culture, the economy, or what we call "the times." My story is not developed in a vacuum. I am what I am because I am immersed in other people's stories and the stories of my time. If I neglect or deny them, I have no personal story to tell. In telling my story, I make sense also of the world I inhabit.[2]

CHAPTER ONE

School Years

Chito's parents believed he was ready for school before his sixth birthday, and the principal of the local state-run elementary school in Imus agreed. But some parents, whose children were not accepted, found out that a five-year-old had been admitted and they complained. The cardinal says his parents did not want to create trouble, so they began looking for another school for their son. They began with schools nearby, gradually widening their search. In the end, Chito ended up at the private St. Andrew's School in Paranaque, more than sixteen rough-road miles from home. The school was run by Belgian members of the Congregation of the Immaculate Heart of Mary, commonly known as the Scheut Missionaries. At the time, the education system in the Philippines was organized around six years of elementary school followed by four years of secondary school. Students generally graduated at the age of sixteen.

Not attending the local public school turned out to be "providential," the cardinal said, "because in addition to what I received from my parents, I got formal religion classes. And early on, the Belgian missionaries instilled in us discipline; focus; frugal, simple living; and a missionary spirit. And I'm very thankful for that foundational formation we got from them."

As a senior, Chito was fifteen years old. "I was in my final year of high school when martial law was declared and, painful as it was, the priests cancelled the junior-senior prom, cancelled all the fancy clothing for graduation—we just had Mass in our school uniform—and of course we rebelled. But we were called to a meeting and the priest explained these are hard times, we don't know where the country is heading, we don't want to impose on your parents additional burdens. So you should learn how to support your parents and your country. For adolescent minds, you know, it was one of our big days, and they were depriving us of it. But they were firm."

Almost until the very end of high school, Chito was convinced that his future was in medicine. He says he was a good Catholic boy and went to Mass every Sunday. But partly because he went to a Catholic school in another town, he was not particularly involved in the life of the Imus parish. "Then came the invasive intrusion in my life! Toward the end of my third year in high school, the Knights of Columbus council in my local parish started the Columbian Squires—kind of the junior members of the Knights of Columbus." His father was a Knight and the elder Tagle and other members of the Imus council decided their sons would be the first Squires. "I was forced to join it," the cardinal said. He knew the names of some of the other boys, but he was not friends with them since he did not go to school with them. "I was an outsider. I knew that I would not have fun. But it was expected of us, so I joined. I think the group saw how I was withdrawing from them, how I dragged my feet to meetings; they elected me president! And I accepted and

I took it seriously. It was a good move on their part. It was also in a way an action of God; it allowed me to get out of my shell and be creative."

The spiritual director of the Squires was a newly ordained priest, Fr. Redentor Corpuz, whom the cardinal describes as "young, energetic, and adventurous." Just eleven years older than Chito, Corpuz was into music and sports, and the young Squires quickly formed a bond with him. "Since he was the spiritual director and I was the president, we spent a lot of time talking to each other," the cardinal said. "I would say he was my first adult friend."

Involvement in the Squires added a new dimension to Chito's parish life and his connections to his peers in Imus. The Squires helped with parish fundraising projects and "we got involved in programs for the street children and the children of informal settlers, the squatters, in the slums; we would organize Christmas parties for them. We also organized sports and cultural events for the youth." In a short span of time, the Squires became friends and Chito's fear "that I would remain an alien" was put to rest.

Chito's parents, whom he describes as "bank employees, who were able to gain some promotions through hard work," would have been able to afford the tuition at St. Andrew's; nevertheless he always was awarded scholarships. "My whole educational journey was marked by people helping me through scholarships—from grade school to the doctoral level. I was always on scholarship, and they came from people who I do not know." The donors "didn't want recognition, they just wanted to help." The cardinal said he tries to repay them by imitating their generosity in continuing to teach at the archdiocesan seminary in Manila and at the Loyola School of Theology where he had earned his master's degree. Jesuit Fr. Jose V. C. Quilongquilong, president of the school of theology, said the cardinal's classes are popular and always full. He also said that while everyone knows the cardinal has an impossible schedule, Tagle always sends a formal note asking to be excused from the faculty meetings he cannot make. Quilongquilong said he has told the cardinal repeatedly that such notes are not necessary, but the cardinal insists that as a faculty member he will follow all the rules in the faculty handbook, including formally asking to be excused from those meetings. Asked why he continues to teach and how he manages with his schedule, the cardinal said, "I am the product of so many generous people, why would I not allow that gift to be given to other people? I realize that what I am now is the fruit of the common effort of so many people—my family, my teachers, and so many people I do not know—forming one community of love and service."

Some of the scholarships he received came from the Knights of Columbus. In 1973, when he was about to enter the Ateneo and the seminary, the Knights awarded him a scholarship for four years. Attending his first-ever Supreme Convention of the Knights of Columbus in 2012, he told the thousands gathered in Anaheim, CA, "My belonging to the group brought me closer to the church and to the call to mission."

While the Squires were active in parish life and striving to be good Catholics, they still were normal young men. When asked if Chito had a girlfriend in those years, the cardinal responded, "I had friends. Of course I thought I would get married and have children." Describing life outside school and church, he said, "We were always in disco houses. I was part of a gang of girls and boys. We would sneak out of the house to go to the discos and parties. But, really, nothing serious developed in those years. You can

call it group dates. We were fourteen, fifteen years old."
Interestingly enough, while there were some flirtations between members of the group and chatter among members
about the potential for various couples ending up together,
no marriages ever occurred between group members. "It
was like we treated each other as brothers and sisters. In
the end, after all the teasing and pairing, it was really like
an extended family. It was like there was an unspoken rule:
no one should get married because you are like brothers
and sisters. We had a gathering a few years ago and we
laughed and laughed because those that we thought would
end up together—that there were possibilities—didn't."

Asked if his mother is disappointed he didn't become a
doctor and get married and give her grandchildren, or if she
is proud that he is a cardinal, he responded, "One thing that
I appreciate even now is that even though my parents had
their own dreams for me and my brother, they fully re-
spected our decisions. Especially my mother, she has that
spiritual side to her that makes her see God's hand in something that is not in accord with her plans. She can accept it
as maybe God has another plan."

Jesuit Fr. Daniel Huang, regional assistant for Asia-Pacific
at the Jesuit headquarters and former provincial of the Philippines, first crossed paths with Chito at the Ateneo's com-
mencement ceremonies in 1973 when Chito graduated with
his bachelor's degree summa cum laude and Huang was a
first-year university student. He said, "For graduations there
is a custom of having a younger student as an usher. You go
on stage and get your medal, then you go to your parents
and the usher carries the medal and your parents put it on
you. I was his usher. But we didn't know each other then."

That changed in 1979 when Chito was doing his graduate
theology studies in Manila and Danny was a pre-novice, about

to enter the Jesuits. "I was assigned to a poor parish near the Ateneo, St. Joseph the Worker in Marikina. He was directing the choir, and I was training the basses. We became friends." At the time, neither had been ordained to the priesthood.

President Ferdinand Marcos's imposition of martial law was part of the environment as the two studied and engaged in pastoral work. Both were involved in social action to the extent that their superiors approved. But the work in the parish was "pastoral action rather than political action. We both had our different political involvements, but the parish was about working with and learning from the poor," Huang says. "One of the things I learned from Chito from that experience was the value of humor and presence, being with and sharing life, making friends. Our work was the normal parish task of working with the choir but Chito wasn't just teaching music, he was visiting homes, making friends, having no differences, being close to people—and always with humor—sharing jokes and sharing meals. My own background was not like his; at that time I was discovering for myself what being close to the poor meant. I came from a more sheltered background, and Chito was very good about helping me bridge the cultural divide."

Chito was ordained to the priesthood in 1982. Huang said, "I was a novice, and I remember crying because my novice master wouldn't let me go his ordination. I was twenty-two years old. He was such an attractive personality."

Three years after his ordination, armed with his bachelor's degree in philosophy from the Ateneo and his master's degree in theology from the Loyola School of Theology, Fr. Chito was sent in 1985 to The Catholic University of America to earn his licentiate and doctorate in theology.

One of his professors in Washington, the one who would become his doctoral director, was Fr. Joseph A. Komonchak, now professor emeritus of theology and religious studies. The professor said of his former student, "I found him very open, obviously a very young priest. He was somewhat shy I would say. Humble. Never paraded around, but also one of the most intelligent and bright students that I had in forty-five years of teaching."

Although supported by scholarships and grants, Chito also was a work-study student. Komonchak said, "Catholic University isn't the wealthiest university around," so when money got tight, Chito "went over to the library and got a job. He also worked in parishes and for the Filipino community—he was all over the place giving talks for them."

On the evening before Archbishop Tagle became a cardinal, Jesuit Fr. Catalino Arevalo, his mentor as a theologian and the person who referred him to Catholic University, told the *Philippine Daily Inquirer* that because his protégé did not introduce himself as a priest when he went to the library, he was assigned to do "dirty work," carrying books and boxes until they found out he was a priest and gave him a less physical job. "When his mother found out, she cried. The Tagles are not very wealthy but they have some money. Both mother and father worked for Equitable Bank. They could have sent him more money" or his brother who was working in Virginia could have helped, "but Chito did not tell his brother. He did his work quietly. He did not want to burden other people. Later on, while I was talking with him, he said he found it quite hard doing his studies while trying to earn the money he needed. This is the kind of person he is," Arevalo said.

Arevalo also identified Huang as a promising theologian and convinced the young priest's superiors to send him to Catholic University as well. "So I arrived in 1989—and this is just a little sign of who Chito was—he was in Brescia

[Italy] doing his research, but he had arranged that his brother would take care of me," Huang said. "I, of course, was with the Jesuit community, but he asked his brother to make sure that I got good Filipino meals and that I be introduced to their family and network of cousins in Washington, DC. It was just a little thing, but so thoughtful; he wanted to make sure that I would be welcomed."

"One of the things that struck me very much, even when he was studying, was his simplicity. He didn't have a religious order to take care of him, and the diocese he was from wasn't a wealthy diocese, so he had to work in the library part-time. He made so many friends there. For his ordination as a bishop and when he received his *pallium* (at the Vatican as archbishop of Manila), people from Catholic U came. He had this amazing gift for making friends and creating loyalty," Huang continued.

In addition to studying and working in the library in Washington, "he made it a point to work at Mother Teresa's shelter for AIDS patients. He regularly volunteered there in addition to all the academic stuff and the pastoral work we would do with Filipino families. He did it quietly, without fanfare. It was just him. He insisted that somehow there would be some connection to the poor" even while working on his doctorate. The pressure of academic work, earning money for his keep, and engaging in ministry did not seem to be a problem, Huang continued. "Chito is very disciplined, extremely disciplined. He did his work and pastoral work as well. It's clear your main work is your studies and Chito did that very well; he was very focused. But he did the pastoral work to keep alive his priesthood, to keep in touch with people. It was a disciplined way of life: you study and, to make sure you don't forget what you are a priest for, you do other things."

Komonchak said he was not surprised in 1997 when Pope John Paul II gave Fr. Tagle a five-year appointment to the International Theological Commission, a body that advises the Congregation for the Doctrine of the Faith. Pope Benedict, then Cardinal Joseph Ratzinger, was president of the commission when Tagle served on it. "I wasn't surprised because I knew how talented he was," says Komonchak, who believed his student should use his talents as a professional theologian. "When he went back to the Philippines after he finished his doctorate, he was given several jobs, any one of which would have tired a normal person out," he said. In fact, Chito's former doctoral director said, "I was about to write to Cardinal Sin in Manila and tell him, 'This man has the chance of being the best theologian in Asia and one of the best theologians in the world. In order for him to do that, he has to have time to read and write and do research. And he's got so many jobs.' And besides that, he was being asked to go talk to every convent of nuns. I said, 'He has to be given the time to do this.' Before I could write the letter, I got notice from Chito that the apostolic delegate had told him that the pope wanted to make him a bishop." His appointment as bishop of Imus was announced in October 2001, and Tagle was ordained a bishop on December 12 by Cardinal Sin.

Komonchak said, "Chito's first reaction was, 'I never wanted to be a bishop.' And I said that the true meaning of vocation is the church calling you to something. He didn't really have a choice I suppose. You don't turn that down. But it was never his plan for himself. He was never an ambitious man." While Chito is not the academic theologian his mentor thought he could be, Komonchak said that what the cardinal does "is pastoral theology in the best sense. Pastoral theology is the study of how the church comes to be and how it acts and that's what he's engaged in. He's helping the church be something different by the way he preaches and what he preaches about."

Huang, who taught with Tagle at the Loyola School of Theology, says that as a professor, his friend always received the best evaluations. "The thing is, he's got depth; he's got clarity. Theology is *scientia et sapientia*—knowledge and wisdom. He reads, is prepared, but he also has *sapientia*, which bridges theology and life, doctrine and life, the mind and the heart. So in his teaching, he is very clear about history, about concepts; he has the scientific aspect, but at the same time, he's never forgotten the wisdom aspect, which is: What does this mean for life? How does this truth touch the heart and transform the life of the person hearing it? I think it's always been something of that sort with him. I think it's partially because his natural environment is a pastoral one. The fact that he's not a university-based theology professor does not mean that he's any less rigorous, but it means his typical audience is different, which has shaped the way he's communicated. He's not arguing with academics primarily —although he can do that very well—but his primary audience has always been the people of God. The locus of theology in Asia is not primarily at the university at this point—maybe we need more of that—but the locus, at least in the Philippines, is the people. A lot is shaped by whom your conversation partners are. And the theologians are trying to do theology for the life of the church, rather than for academic journals. So that's why I think his theology is closer to the fathers of the church than to the university," Huang said. The material that forms the basis of patristic theology consists of the homilies and pastoral letters the early church theologians wrote as instruction and inspiration, not as isolated reflections on theological questions. He continued,

"You cannot say the theology of the fathers of the church is any less theology, it's just a different mode."

While heading an archdiocese the size of Manila is already more than a full-time job, Cardinal Tagle continues his weekly television reflection on the coming Sunday's Mass readings and serves on several Vatican councils. And the cardinal continues to teach theology "because he loves it, first of all," Huang said. "And he's a great communicator. I think it's also partially to keep himself mentally alert in being forced to prepare and to read and to think. It's where he's able to maintain and keep alive that intellectual aspect of his life. He likes teaching. I think other people play golf or basketball to relax, and he teaches. But I also think it gives him a chance to think."

Archbishop Tagle told Canada's Salt + Light Television in a 2012 interview, "Good theology has a pastoral thrust; good theology isn't meant to satisfy the curiosity of the theologian. It is not just a way to test one's talent and creativity. Theology is at the service of the faith of the people. If theology is distant from the concerns of the people, their questions, their world, I don't think it will be good theology. And good theology should be understandable to people and it should aid them, help them deepen their encounter with the Lord."

CHAPTER TWO

Vocation

From a young age, Chito Tagle's vocation path was set: university, medical school, and life as a doctor. Probably married with children. He never played priest as a boy and was never an altar server in his parish. In his last year of high school, a priest to whom he was not particularly close encouraged him to take the exams for a scholarship at the Jesuit-run Ateneo de Manila University. As it turned out, part of the exams was for potential seminarians, but Chito did not discover that until he was in the exam hall faced with the questionnaire.

"I grew up conditioned, in a way, to become a medical doctor, and I liked the idea," he said. He enjoyed math and science and, he admitted, as a boy he was attracted to the esteem that comes with being a doctor. But he also liked the intellectual challenge of getting into a good university and a good medical school and passing all the exams. Chito's godfather, his mother's younger brother, was a physician, and he would send his young godson medical books. "At twelve, thirteen years old I was already reading medical books to prepare for the entrance exams for medical schools."

The prestige was not primarily connected to potential income, but had more to do with admiration and leadership in the community. "I remember with fondness the family doctors we had in our village, our town," Tagle said. "You could call on them anytime. They were lovable, compassionate. They were members of the family; they knew the history of the family. You didn't have to go to the clinic, because they would come to the house. They were like fathers to us. So, reflecting on this, I see the service, the selflessness of doctors and also the prestige captured my imagination."

"In hindsight, I guess at that time, without using the word *vocation*, the dream of becoming a medical doctor provided some direction for me, a goal I wanted to pursue," he said.

Although all of his formal education before university was under the direction of the Congregation of the Immaculate Heart of Mary, known as the Scheut Missionaries, he said he never considered becoming one of them. "I admired them, but I was also afraid of them; they were disciplinarians and they would call you to their offices to ask you about your behavior." The missionaries, most of whom were Belgians, "taught us, in a rudimentary way, some of their practices. Every morning at the beginning of class we had to recite not only morning prayer, but also the morning offering. We had to recite the Ten Commandments, the commandments of the church—it was like, through memorizing, it became part of your daily consciousness." He had what he considers basic formation in the faith at home and "very solid, very missionary formation" from the priests at school.

It was only during the third year of high school—when the students were fourteen or fifteen years old—that the missionaries distributed promotional material about the priesthood and religious life. "We read them, but I did not take any of them seriously and, in fact, I found some of them quite strange," he said. The cardinal still remembers phrases from the pamphlets like: "The hands of the priest are different from ordinary hands" or "As a priest, you will be a different person." Most vocations material today has found other ways to say the same thing, but the concepts the phrases were trying to describe are still part of church teaching about an "ontological change" or "an indelible spiritual character" that takes place within a man at ordination.

Chito was in high school in the early 1970s. The Second Vatican Council had ended in 1965, and its teachings were just beginning to be implemented around the globe. The language used to describe everything from the church as a whole to its individual ministers was changing.

One priest who was ahead of the curve was Fr. Redentor Corpuz, Chito's friend and assistant pastor at the Tagle family's parish in Imus. Visiting the Tagle family, Corpuz noticed the Scheut Missionaries' pamphlets. He asked Chito why he had them, and the boy explained that his entire class was given the material. Father Corpuz flipped through the brochures and said, " 'Oh my, these are old-fashioned materials,' and he said this is not the way to speak of priesthood now. I told him I had looked at it, and I didn't pay much attention. Then he said, 'You are too young to think about these things, about priesthood; you're too young. If you are going to make a decision about your future, especially if it is related to the priesthood, talk with me. See me and we will talk about it.' " And Chito agreed.

At the beginning of Chito's last year of high school, Corpuz was transferred and given his own parish even though he was only twenty-six years old at the time. Chito and a couple other teens from Imus helped Corpuz move to his remote parish, about a three- or four-hour drive away at that time.

Chito and two other members of the Columbian Squires stayed with Corpuz for three days, helping him unpack and get his first look at the village and his first encounters with the people. "We walked around with him; he introduced himself to the people from house to house. And we saw the poverty of the place.

"I remember distinctly my emotions at the time. I felt sad this friend of mine would be far away," the cardinal continued. "It was one of the poorest parishes of the diocese. The houses were literally shanties and the rectory was some sort of big 'nipa'—a hut with leaves for a roof. And you'd see pigs roaming around the roads. It was a fishing community and very poor, very poor." The poverty of the village made a big impression on Chito. "I think I was turning fifteen at the time, or just fifteen. And one of the thoughts that came to me looking around and at my priest friend was the question: Why would he waste his life here? What would make a person waste his talents on a community that will not be able to give him anything in return . . . in the sense of good living conditions, money. Is it worth it? I was wondering why. What are the reasons for a person to waste his life for others? I felt sad for my friend because at the time that was my perspective—what a waste of life. But at the same time, I admired him all the more. I admired him, not with an understanding of what was going on, but I admired him."

In Imus, Corpuz was replaced by a new assistant priest, one Chito did not like as much. "There wasn't anything wrong with him, but he wasn't as friendly; he wasn't too accommodating. So our group, the Squires, sort of distanced ourselves from this new spiritual director," but he quickly added, "we didn't fight with him." The new priest was the one who started talking about priesthood and asking Chito about his plans. "I said, 'Um, well, I'm going to medical school.'" And the priest said that the Ateneo de Manila, one of the most prestigious—and expensive—universities in the Philippines had scholarships available, but a rigorous series of exams and interviews was necessary to win one. Although the Ateneo did not have a medical school at the time, the priest pointed out that the university was so prestigious that if Chito did premed there and did well, he could get into any medical school he wanted. "I said, especially if there is a scholarship, who would not want to enter the Ateneo de Manila university? Very few could afford it. So I said yes."

Along with other students taking the exams, Chito was given lodging on campus at the diocesan seminary, which was staffed by the Jesuits.

"Then came the first set of exams. And I was surprised because one of the questions was: 'Type of vocation.' So I went to the proctor and said, 'What do I put here?' And he said, 'priesthood.' And I said, 'Why priesthood?' He said, 'This is the entrance exam for the seminary.'" When Cardinal Tagle told this story, sitting in a small reception room at the Philippine seminary in Rome, he was laughing so hard that he was almost wheezing. Young men applying to the seminary in Manila were required to take two exams: one for the seminary and one for the university, where most of their classes would be. Candidates for the priesthood were accepted only if they passed both exams.

When the proctor told Chito what the exam was for, he said, "I was fuming mad. But I did not know how to get home. I would have gotten lost. So I had to stay on." And he finished the tests. As soon as he was back home he went straight to the parish. "I confronted the priest, 'Why did you do that?' He said, 'I just want you to widen your horizons. You are always thinking of medical school; you don't take seriously the other options.'" However, the priest explained that if Chito passed the university entrance exam he could still study biology at the Ateneo and continue his preparations for medical school.

More than forty years later, the cardinal said, "I was angry. But he succeeded in some regard. It confused me. It brought me to that question: 'What do I really want to do with my life? Am I really set on becoming a doctor?'" His experiences at his parish, in school, with Corpuz, and at the priest's poor parish—"they all came back and added to the confusion," he said. "But I was still clinging to the dream of becoming a doctor. It brought me confusion. And what confused me all the more was that I discovered in my heart, as the weeks went on, there was a hidden desire or wish to pass the exams. And I got disturbed all the more because it made me ask if what I really wanted all along was to become a priest. Was that an option?"

Chito did not tell his parents or his teachers that he had been fooled into taking the seminary entrance exam. But it was something he was pondering and praying about. After a few days, the exam results were sent to Chito's school. The principal, a Belgian missionary, asked Chito why he was receiving mail from San Jose Seminary. "I told him the story, and I opened the letter. As I expected, the result was no." Looking back, the cardinal is impressed with how serious and how accurate the tests and interviews were. His confusion had been clear. "They said you are not ready for seminary life. You need to mature, to make a decision." The principal asked Chito if he had any interest in the priesthood. "And I said, 'No, Father, I am confused right now because I really want to become a doctor, but then this trick was played on me.' And he said, 'Maybe you can talk to the vocation director of the diocese and he can help you make sense of this.' I said I don't even know him."

While Chito failed the seminary entrance exam, he did pass the test for admittance to the university and was awarded a scholarship that would help him do his premed studies at the Ateneo. But was that what he really should study? The confusion remained. He had been used to getting up very early to get ready for school, which was in a town sixteen miles away. "So at this time, I would wake up early and be in the church in before five o'clock, and I would spend time before the Blessed Sacrament asking God to help me." He said his prayer was simple: "Please, I don't know what to do."

But there was a time pressure. He had to decide whether or not he was going to the Ateneo and, if so, where he would live. His parents wanted to know where he planned on doing his premed studies. Still conflicted between priesthood and medicine, Chito went to the diocesan vocations director and laid out the whole story. His advice was that if Chito was serious about entering the seminary, he should go to the rector of the seminary and tell him the whole truth, which is what he did.

The rector was sympathetic about Chito feeling anger over being tricked into taking the seminary exam unprepared and about how that led the young man to wrestle over his vocation. But the rector still told Chito there was no place in the seminary for him. The cardinal said the rector told him, "If you had a vocation, that would have manifested in the exam, even if you had not been fooled or tricked into it." Chito was not convinced. He made several visits to the university in the following weeks, preparing to begin as a university student. Every time he was on campus, he would go see the rector and ask to be allowed to take the exam again. The rector seemed so sure that the exam could detect a vocation that Chito thought it could help him know for sure. But the rector refused.

Chito had to return to campus a while later to pay his registration fee as a regular student. At that point he had decided that four visits to the rector were enough. He wasn't going back and would not knock on that door again. Instead, he went directly to the cashier's office to pay, joining a long line of other students.

The Jesuit who proctored the exam Chito had failed walked by and said, "You are Tagle, right?" The Jesuit said he had heard from the rector about how persistent Chito was being about retaking the exam. Chito replied that he had given that up and would focus on biology. The Jesuit, who also was on the university admissions board, invited Chito into his office. "He interviewed me a bit and asked me if I knew any priests. So I mentioned the name of my friend and of this priest who played a trick on me. They were his former classmates in theology! He asked me, 'Do you know how to pray?' I said I go to the Blessed Sacrament chapel every day, especially during these past weeks. He said, 'Okay. Just a minute.' He made a phone call and returned and said, 'I just talked to the rector. We'll give it a try. We accept you in the seminary—for a semester. You'll be on probation, we'll observe you and then we'll see.'"

He also let Chito know that he was already behind. The seminarians had begun their orientation and were about to begin a retreat before university classes began. The Jesuit told Chito to report to the seminary first thing in the morning. "And I said, 'But my parents don't know.' I hadn't told them anything. He said, 'Call them.'"

Leaving campus that day, Chito passed by the seminary and the rector was standing outside. He told Chito, "You had your first lesson: if you want to pursue something, pray hard and work hard."

Chito got home and finally told his parents the whole story. "It was a letdown for them, I know. They really wanted me to be a doctor." He said he had not told them anything earlier because "I was a bit afraid to tell them, but mostly I didn't know what to tell them. I was not sure I wanted it or that I would be accepted. I didn't know if this was just a passing feeling or just part of my admiration for someone. Was I just mimicking or sort of idolizing someone and pretending that I could be him? I was not sure, so what could I tell my parents? What was more certain was that I wanted to be a doctor."

The cardinal said his parents listened to him and did not try to dissuade him. Although he is not certain the story was true, "somebody told me that when I entered the seminary, for some Sundays my father did not go to church. I don't know if he was reacting or showing that priest that he had not liked what he had done" in tricking his son and planting the priesthood idea in his head.

Of all the first-year seminarians at San Jose Seminary that year, Chito was the only one who had not attended a minor seminary. His classmates already were familiar with a seminary routine and even the seminary lingo. Chito, on the other hand, said he "would get nervous every time the bell rang . . . 'What's that for?'" But Chito was a serious student, dedicated to his studies, and he felt the added pressure of being on probation, so he knuckled down. "My mindset then was that if I'm not meant for this, if this is not for me, I can pursue my other dream. It's not like it was the only life available to me; I knew I had other options. But I should say I invested in that life, especially in the first semester, because I really wanted to know. At the end of the first semester, I presented myself to the rector. 'So, Father, should I return for the second semester?' He asked why I was asking. I said you told me I was in for a semester. He said, 'Oh forget about it, just continue.' So then I was a full-blooded seminarian."

The only real negative reaction came from Chito's Chinese grandfather—his mother's father and a convert to Catholicism. "He told me point blank, 'I do not understand this priesthood thing, and I'm not particularly excited to have a grandson becoming priest.' The Chinese are very pragmatic about good jobs and family. But he said, 'If you want to become a priest, I want you to be a good priest. No mediocrity!'" The cardinal said that "when I feel tired and lazy" he goes back in his mind to that conversation with his grandfather and "it strengthens me. . . . I can hear him saying, 'I don't understand what being a cardinal is, but I want you to be a good one!'" His family, he said, made it clear all along that the seminary and eventual priesthood was not something they were pushing Chito into, and in fact they had had another dream for him. In some ways, he said, his parents' attitude was, "You did it by yourself, you hid it from us, and informed us only a few hours before entering. Now you take full responsibility for it."

"The way things unfolded," he said, even if his parents "did not like my decision to enter the seminary, they supported it, they accepted it as God's plan, and now they see it was God's plan. Imagine," he said, laughing, "I end up being a cardinal! So it became part of my parents' contemplation of beholding what God is doing not only for me, but for the family, and they are very grateful to God. There are many things about my life that they don't understand, but they've always been there. And they use this as an occasion, as parents of a cardinal, as a way of getting closer to God, beholding and keeping and cherishing things in their hearts like the Blessed Mother."

Chito was fifteen years old when he entered the seminary. He says that if a youth that age came up to him today asking to be admitted to the seminary, "I would discourage that person too. The seminary exam was accurate. They were right in discouraging me. But they also had to contend with the fact that they accept younger boys to minor seminaries, so what is to prevent them from accepting a fifteen-year-old who has already completed high school?"

Chito also had to break the news to his friends at home, the same friends he would sneak out of the house with to go to discos. "They were shocked," he said, but at least when they heard the whole story they realized Chito had not been keeping a secret from them. One of his friends, a former seminarian, was angry and hurt that Chito hadn't spoken to him about it. But in the end, all the friend said was to remember, " 'You can enter the seminary and you [can] leave.' I told him I knew that."

A similar reaction came from Corpuz, who earlier had extracted a promise that Chito would discuss with him any thoughts about maybe becoming a priest. On the seminarians' first free weekend that semester, Chito's parents drove him to Corpuz's village. The priest said he knew Chito would enjoy seminary life, but he told the young man, "keep your options open." Eventually, Chito would become Corpuz's bishop.

The cardinal said he didn't apologize to Fr. Corpuz until, as bishop, he spoke at a celebration for the priest's sixty-fifth birthday, a celebration that came only a few weeks before Fr. Corpuz unexpectedly died of a heart attack. But the lessons he learned from the priest about "wasting" one's life with the poor have stayed with him.

Discussing how to train and mold priests for the new evangelization, Cardinal Tagle told a gathering of the Federation of Asian Bishops' Conferences, "In many cultures, becoming a seminarian is a step up from the rest of humanity. Becoming a deacon is two steps above the rest of humanity. Becoming a priest? Wow! You belong more to heaven than earth. You are perceived as a journeyer with the angels and not a traveler with human beings."[1] But, the cardinal added (and repeats every time he ordains a priest), priesthood is a call to be authentically concerned about others, to console those who are hurting, and to reconcile people with God.

Presenting the Italian edition of his book *Easter People* in Rome in 2013, he told reporters, "In my mind, Luis Antonio Gokim Tagle is a simple person called by God to serve as a simple priest in a simple parish with ordinary people. But the Lord had other things in mind."

CHAPTER THREE

Humility and Simplicity

"I really am amazed at what God has done to me and for me through other people," Cardinal Tagle said. His family, the Scheut Missionaries, the Jesuits at his seminary and at the Ateneo de Manila University—and especially the poor—have taught him that simplicity is not primarily about where he lives, what he wears, or what he owns. It's a matter of the heart, which is reflected first of all in the way he treats other people and only later in material things.

Simplicity is a lesson learned gradually and begins with the smallest things. Cardinal Tagle said he believes his approach to material things and to stewardship began with his elementary school textbooks. The parents did not buy the books for their children; the school provided them. But the missionaries made it clear to those young boys that they had an obligation to care for the books and keep them pristine for the next generation of students.

The Jesuits at his university and at the San Jose Seminary taught the young man the spiritual roots of simplicity and how it reflects one's relationship to God and serves as a form of solidarity with the poor. The Jesuits taught prayer and discernment, "the freedom of the heart from other attachments," and how that detachment is necessary to be truly of service to the church and society. "It's not just about activism, having something to do, or riding with the fashion," Tagle said, "but coming from a spirituality."

They were not easy lessons to learn, and they were not lessons confined to a classroom. "Ohhhh, how I suffered!" the cardinal said. The spiritual director would ask: "'Why did you choose this? Was that the only option? Why did you not choose this? Did you think about the following of Christ in this choice?' Things like that." The questions were designed to help the seminarians think about how everything they did fit into the way they were following Christ or imitating Christ. That kind of reflection, repeated over years in the seminary, is something that sticks, he said. "I still have it."

Soon after the 2013 conclave that elected the Jesuit Pope Francis—the first papal election Tagle participated in and one that many in the media actually thought had a chance of bringing him to the papacy—the cardinal was back at the Jesuit-run Ateneo de Manila University to speak at the graduation ceremony. He focused on the spiritual lessons taught by St. Ignatius, the founder of the Jesuits, and on how the graduates would honor their Jesuit education by striving to find God in all things. "A mind and heart with a clear purpose seeks God," he told them. "Perhaps it can also be said that God wants to be found in the times when we feel our purpose is unclear. In the times when we feel we can't see him, perhaps he's the one searching for you. . . . When someone comes up to me and says, 'I feel lost,' I don't always know what to say. Sometimes though, I just say, 'Just wait to be found. As you are searching for God, God is searching for you.'"[1]

All Christians, he told the graduates, are called to strive for "that profound humility that made St. Ignatius open to anything that the church would want him to embrace—that depth of seeing God, hearing God, loving God in all, and following God even in the darkness of your life, hoping and believing that the One you are searching is searching for you." When life is difficult, when you seem lost, he told the students, "strength, light and fortitude" come from knowing that God is there, searching for you as well.

Jesuit Fr. Daniel Huang, longtime friend of the cardinal's and former rector of San Jose Seminary, said the Jesuits at Ateneo are clear that they are forming diocesan priests, but that they are doing so with Ignatian spirituality. "We believe Ignatian spirituality isn't just for the Jesuits, but for others as well," he said. "It's very strong in the formation. We still have a year, which we called the spiritual-pastoral formation year, where the seminarians live in the Jesuit novitiate, and Chito did that as well. They do the spiritual exercises—the full spiritual exercises of thirty days. Then there are the values you get constantly: the 'magis' or the more; doing things for the greater glory of God; discernment and freedom." As a priest and rector of Our Lady of the Pillar Seminary in Imus from 2002–11, Chito introduced the spiritual exercises to his own seminary and "he's been directing the spiritual exercises for thirty years," Huang says. When Jesuit Fr. Antonio Spadaro conducted the first long interview with Pope Francis, an interview published in Jesuit journals around the world in September 2013, Cardinal Tagle told Huang "he was surprised by how much he resonated with it, precisely because it was Ignatian; it made him think again how Ignatian his own spirituality is." The pope and the cardinal "have the same instincts, in many ways the same gifts: closeness to the poor, natural simplicity, integrity, the gift of communication. If there is one thing Chito is, it's a communicator. He has an amazing presence. There's clearly a depth of theological thinking, but he is able to communicate in the language of people," his friend said.

In an interview for this book, Cardinal Tagle said that in high school and especially in college and in seminary, he learned "simplicity as an evangelical value and as an act of solidarity with the poor." They were lessons missionaries, priests, and nuns taught their students in the years after the Second Vatican Council, particularly in the Philippines after Ferdinand Marcos declared martial law in 1972. It was a time, the cardinal said, "when people were deprived of freedoms, and the poor were becoming poorer while there was an elite who had all the power, there were the dictators enjoying all the goods."

Chito was used to a simple lifestyle. Although many good-hearted people think that now that he is archbishop of Manila and the dignity of his office calls for a bit more affluence, it clearly goes against his background and training even when it comes to ecclesiastical and liturgical clothing and adornments. As he was growing up and preparing for ordination, the Scheut Missionaries, the Jesuits, and just the mood in the church and in the country meant such accoutrements had little or no importance. "Even now," the cardinal said, "I keep forgetting my pectoral cross. I always miss one or two items of the whole package. It's something I have to learn. But for me, it's not just carelessness; it's rooted in thinking 'Do I really need these trappings? Do they define you as a Christian, as a minister? Are they the defining characteristics of a church?' But there is also the apostolic dimension, how in your little ways your simplicity can lead to solidarity and sharing with those who do not have enough."

When he was named archbishop of Manila in 2011, the *National Catholic Reporter* ran an article that included the following story.

Not long after Tagle arrived in Imus (in 2001), a small chapel located in a run-down neighborhood was waiting for a priest to say Mass for a group mostly made up of day laborers at around 4 a.m. Eventually a youngish cleric showed up on a cheap bicycle, wearing simple clothes and ready to start the Mass. An astonished member of the congregation realized it was the new bishop, and apologized that they hadn't prepared a better welcome. Tagle said it was no problem; he got word late the night before that the priest was sick, and decided to say the Mass himself.[2]

The cardinal said he still is astonished that people find that story so surprising. And he hurried to point out that he did not arrive on a bicycle, but on what Filipinos call a "tricycle," a motorized rickshaw that is one of the most common forms of public transportation in the country. "I had to rush to this village chapel since I was available," the cardinal explained. "The priest got sick, so why not take over? What I found interesting was not the experience, but how people right before the conclave were fascinated by that story. I thought, 'Why was that so interesting?' I could have walked or taken a jeepney or bus."

As a priest, he did not own a car. And for the first year that he was bishop of Imus, he continued taking public transportation. "First of all, I did not have the money to buy a car. And second, I thought it was good for me as a pastor to be close to people. The way I say it is I could smell the Filipinos in the morning, how fresh they were going to work. And I could smell their weariness, their tiredness after work. And I could see what the ordinary people go through, sitting there for hours stuck in traffic, in buses that are not air conditioned; you get exposed to pollution, to the rain, to the heat of the sun. For me, it was a pastoral moment. You are able to interact, people talk to you. Sometimes no one knows you and you are able just to listen to what they're concerned about. It enlarges my world; it broadens my horizons."

That lasted only about a year after he became bishop, though. The priests of the diocese did not mind having a bishop who was one of the people. But they did mind having a bishop who was always late for confirmations, special celebration Masses, and meetings. "So at a certain point, some priests came to me and, in a very friendly way, said, 'Bishop, we appreciate your desire to remain simple and humble, but you're a bishop now. You have a diocese to take care of. On a regular day you have five meetings and two Eucharistic celebrations. We cannot go on this way.'" The cardinal said he took their plea at face value, but also as a warning against the possibility of falling into "spiritual pride: just trying to prove to others that I am humble." The priests believed his ministry was suffering, so he decided it was time to "use the means available," which in this case was a car owned by the seminary. "But the seminary also had its needs. They had the priority (when it came to using the car), and so I ended up with the same problem. Then a priest lent his personal vehicle to me and said he'd use his parish vehicle. But after a week, the parish vehicle got into an accident so he had to reclaim his car." At that point, the vicar general of the diocese got bold. "He said, 'Bishop, enough of this, we will buy a car for the use of the bishop.' And some people helped buy it."

A car was not the only thing he did without in his initial days as a bishop. He told the National Association of Filipino Priests–USA in November 2014 that when he was bishop of Imus he did not have an office or at least not "a room that one could call an office. And I was questioned, 'Bishop, why don't you have an office?' And I said, 'I do.' 'Where?' 'Wherever I am.' Wherever I am I can encounter people and so I hold office there. And, besides, if I have a room that is comfortable, spacious, I might be tempted to stay there. And that's the end of my traveling, my journeying with people."

The pressures to have and use nice things increased when Bishop Tagle was transferred to Manila in 2011 and grew even more when he was named a cardinal by Pope Benedict XVI late in 2012. Although Manila is not historically the first see of the church in the Philippines, the city is the country's capital, and its archbishop has been seen as a leader for decades. Dealing with expectations and avoiding temptation, he said, starts deep inside with prayer and honest self-examination. "Simplicity for me must begin with the person and is not to be measured only by the externals. Simplicity in the sense of remaining humble, remaining connected to people, not living on illusions about yourself, not manipulating people for personal gain. That is a battle that I have to engage in, whether people see it or not. And I believe everyone should grapple with that internally for without that, even if I am in the most austere room, the most austere setting, I remain complex and greedy in my heart and in my mind."

Not long after he was transferred to Manila, he told the Canadian Catholic television channel Salt + Light that he hoped to continue in the line of archbishops of Manila who were prayerful men, strong shepherds, and great defenders of the poor. But the unique qualities of each of them, he said, is a sign of God's grace, and while he wants to be a man of faith, a defender of the poor and a good shepherd, he will do so as himself. "I do not want to be a caricature of anyone, even if they were great," he said. "I was called—not somebody else—to be the archbishop of Manila. And in my weaknesses, in my limitations, in my giftedness, I am Chito and I have to be true to that. And I should learn how to better myself and

I should learn how to use the gifts that the Lord has given me" for the ministry the church has asked of him now.

When people offer him something, which they do often, "first I ask myself whether these things they are offering are really needed. If they are not really needed, either because they are superfluous or we already have something equivalent, then I politely tell them the truth: that while their gifts are beautiful and good, I don't want to put them to waste, and I won't be able to use them," he said. The next step is to suggest other uses for their gift or an alternative gift. "So it becomes an evangelizing moment: 'Don't look at me and my needs alone. There are also other people in the archdiocese in need.' " It can be tricky, he said. He once encouraged benefactors of the seminary to think about other communities they could help as well. "Some resent it, I have to say. But some welcome the challenge, and I rejoice seeing them moving out of the confines of the seminary or the bishop's residence in order to help other people. I have to do it in a discreet way, in an evangelical way, and I use a bit of humor also, in order to touch hearts."

His friend Huang says being a bishop and cardinal has not changed Chito, "it has just given him more responsibilities. He's basically the same person, but in a funnier outfit. I remember when he first became bishop and he had to design a coat of arms, and he was so upset by that. He said, 'I come from a middle-class family and now I have to have a coat of arms,' which is always a sign of nobility. So he used the hat of a Philippine farmer" instead of a bishop's hat on the top of the shield.

Embracing humility and striving each day to ensure it is not the same as being naive or open to manipulation, Huang said. "Chito is his own man. He comes from a province, Cavite, which is known for having people who are tough and hot-tempered. Some of that is in him, as well. He's not a pushover. He's able to reshape things. For example, at formal talks where bishops are involved you always begin, 'Your eminence, your excellencies . . .' Chito always begins by saying, 'My dear friends, people of God, among whom are our beloved shepherds . . . ' It's a little thing, but it's so different from this long list where you get to the laity at the very end. Chito has never done that; he's always managed to greet the bishops, giving them a special place, but always in the wider context of inclusiveness."

Pope Benedict XVI announced during the 2012 Synod of Bishops on new evangelization that he would be making Archbishop Tagle, a synod delegate, a cardinal. Two days before the public announcement, the cardinal recounted, "I received a card in the synod hall with a phone number and a note: 'During the break, please call this number.' I called. It was the Secretary of State (Cardinal Tarcisio Bertone), and he asked me to come to his office at 4:50 p.m. I thought, 'Why not 5:00 p.m.' but, no, he said 4:50, so I thought 'okay.' But the small groups began at 4:00 p.m., so I asked the head of my group, the archbishop of Dublin (Diarmuid Martin) to excuse me at about 4:30 and he said yes. Then I thought, 'Archbishop Martin worked in the Roman Curia for many years,' so I said to him, 'Hey, Archbishop, when a bishop is called to the Secretariat of State, why? What could I have done wrong?' He said, 'Maybe the Holy Father will send you to Syria' because the Holy Father had announced there would be a delegation from the synod who would go to Syria in a sign of solidarity. I thought, 'Ah, I'll represent Asia.' While I was walking from the synod hall to the Secretariat of State, I was thinking, 'I'm going to have to change my plane ticket to go to Damascus.' At 4:50 Bertone said, 'There's a letter from the Holy Father that I would like to read to you.' It had the usual form, but this time, at the part where the Holy Father announces the specific task, it didn't say Syria, but 'cardinal.' I thought, 'Me?' Then Bertone said he would tell the Holy Father that he had informed me. There was no opportunity for questions. The cardinal told me that the next day the pope would make the formal announcement." And then he was dismissed.

"I was very surprised, very surprised. I did not feel worthy of this," the cardinal said. Television stations and newspapers around the world published photos of the cardinal crying as he received his red hat a month later. Several months after that, he told reporters:

> They were the tears of a man who does not understand this visitation—and I still don't. Yesterday, in the Apostolic Palace someone called me "Eminence" and I looked around, "Oh, that's me." I have to remind myself. They were the tears of a man who knows himself, his sins and limits. However, there is a call to which you cannot say no, only yes with love and trust. They also were tears of fear, but also joy, especially when one of my five companions in becoming cardinals said to me, "You're fortunate that your parents are still living and can be here to share this moment of your life." It's true. It's a grace.
>
> In my mind, Luis Antonio Gokim Tagle is a simple person called by God to serve as a simple priest in a simple parish with ordinary people. But the Lord had other things in mind. [As for the tears,] I cry quickly and easily. I don't know if it's a weakness or a strength, but it comes naturally. I don't hide my emotions very easily.

Cardinal Tagle often is moved to tears by the stories of the poor and hurting. But he also sees those people as messengers to him, explaining who God is, who Jesus is, and how, through the Holy Spirit, the Trinity is still active in the world and still speaking to people today. One only has to learn to listen. He continued speaking to the group of reporters:

> I believe the person of Jesus Christ, his style of human relationships, his compassion, his struggle with the God he called "Abba," Father—these experiences Jesus had are present in the contemporary world and we can see parallels between the events in the life of Jesus and events in our lives. The word of God is not abstract; it's not filled with ideas that help us flee the world. No, the Son of God became human, and every human experience resonates with Jesus' experiences. In the absurdity and complexity of our lives, we can see the light in the ministry, death, and resurrection of Jesus, especially the resurrection, which is hope because we know the last chapter of human history: the victory of the Lord, not evil.
>
> The church must rediscover this truth by listening again to the word of God . . . especially in and through the lives of the people of God, particularly the poor, the homeless, the marginalized, migrants, orphans, widows—these people are for me models of hope. To hear them say "God" with a smile on their lips, with patience, perseverance, and joy even amid the misery of their lives, these people are missionaries to me. What wisdom!

It is a wisdom he urges the priests in his archdiocese to learn from. Ordaining three new priests on January 31, 2015, the cardinal began by telling the congregation that while his homily obviously was written with the ordinands in mind, all those who share the same baptism have a "common calling to follow Jesus and to be missionaries in our time, in our world." The lessons drawn from the gospel story of the Good Shepherd, he said, are not only for priests but for anyone who has "a mission, a service of responsibility. Parents, in some ways you are also shepherds. Teachers, you are also shepherds. Businesspeople, you are also shepherds," he told the congregation at the ordination.

> A shepherd is a person who has deep concern for the others. In the end, as far as Jesus is concerned, the heart of the shepherd is the heart that is full of concern for the others. And that concern will be tested. Can you lay down your life for others? Too often people's devotion to their job is determined only by what they can earn doing it. Society, even the church, has experienced so much destruction and pain because of shepherds who lacked concern for the others and were concerned only with pay or other forms of reward. The shepherd consoles his frightened and bewildered sheep. You are not ordained to bring more discomfort, to bring more mourning, to bring more heaviness to lives that are already burdened. With the spirit of the Lord in you, bring his comforting and consoling love. This is one privilege of the ordained. People will open their hearts to you, in confession, in counseling. And you will touch the mystery of their indescribable pain. Many times we saw during the visit of Pope Francis [to the Philippines], he was reduced to being speechless before the pain and suffering of the people. And even in your silence with the spirit that has anointed you, bring comfort, consolation.[3]

Humility is a virtue that needs constant exercise to stay honed, the cardinal said in an interview for this book. "When people give me special treatment, and when I catch myself being tempted to believe I am this special human being, a special gift of God, I say to myself, 'Hey, look, don't forget your beginnings, don't forget your roots.' I'm very happy and grateful to God that those simple people—my parents, my aunts and uncles, my cousins—I'm thankful that they were lower-middle-class families who worked hard and with dignity and their values were in the right place: education, family, church, being good neighbors to others. Just remembering them already makes me humble," the cardinal says.

But there is an even deeper reality that should keep believers humble, a reality the cardinal said he reminds himself of frequently: "Remembering my own humanity, remembering my share of the human condition, I am as ignorant as the rest of humanity on many, many topics. I am as sinful as other people. I can get tired, I can get irritated, I can get biased—all the things that saints and sinners experience are in me. I'm no different from the rest, so why should I think of myself as a cut above the rest? It's basic self-acceptance and a realistic view of myself. And the other thing is if I review, if I look back, I have to admit that many of the good things that have happened to me are not fruits or effects of my initiative or my industry," but gifts that came from others.

CHAPTER FOUR

On Being a Bishop

Being a bishop is not something Chito or his parents ever imagined would happen. And becoming cardinal-archbishop of Manila with its almost three million Catholic faithful was definitely not foreseen. Eight months after his appointment as the thirty-second archbishop of Manila, he told Canada's Salt + Light Television that his predecessors fought for the rights of the poor and were true spiritual leaders of the people.

My goal is to continue this great legacy of faith, this great legacy of shepherding that my predecessors have left behind. Of course, each one was unique. . . . I will study very well the legacy of my predecessors, and I will try my very best to be as good as they were, but also I don't want to lose who I am.

I was trembling before this prospect of being installed as archbishop of Manila, and I continue to tremble now. But in one moment of fear, I was with a former teacher of mine, I ventilated, and he said, "You know, Chito"—they call me Chito—he said, "There are things in the ministry that are constant: you may be in Washington, DC, you may be in

Imus or Manila, but it is the same word of God that you proclaim, the same sacraments, the same service. But you will find something unique in Manila. And Manila will find something unique in you, your person. Share your person with them." And I said, "Yes, that's good to hear."

While it seems nothing could have prepared Chito to be a bishop and cardinal, looking back he does see how a brutally honest comment from a rector when he was in San Jose Seminary had a big impact on his approach to shepherding a flock, whether that be a parish or a diocese or an archdiocese. The cardinal said, "At the end of my third year of theology—before my last year—he told me, 'Don't expect to be ordained next year.' He gave me a [lot of feedback]: 'You are very efficient and you do your work well, but you can be a Hitler, you can be domineering if you want something done well. Because you aim at perfection,' he said, 'the seminarians just rely on you and they aren't developed.' When I heard that, I was so hurt. But now as a bishop, as a cardinal, even as a priest, I think that's one big lesson I treasure. Now I think I'm moving to the other extreme—even in discussions—I have an idea and I wait for people, thinking maybe they will say it. Thanks to that rector, I've become more accommodating, more appreciative of the gifts of others, more consultative, more participatory in my approach to projects."

Despite what that rector had said, Chito was ordained to the priesthood on February 27, 1982, for the Diocese of Imus. For three years he served simultaneously at parishes in the diocese and on the staff of the diocesan seminary, where eventually he became rector. He also taught philosophy and theology at the Divine Word and San Carlos Seminaries and at the Loyola School of Theology where he had studied. In October 2001, at the age of forty-four, he was named bishop of Imus, a ministry he carried out for ten years before being transferred to Manila.

While his rector's admonitions were blunt and helpful, the cardinal said he also sees his family life as an inspirational model for what he strives to be as a pastor and bishop. While growing up, he and his family lived with his great-grandmother; their home was the focal point and gathering place for the extended clan—his own grandmother and all her siblings, his father and all his siblings, and all the cousins of varying degrees. "Looking back now, I realize that my immediate family played a role within the extended family, it was some sort of a visible symbol of unity, it was the reference point for a clan. So I grew up experiencing that. Once I became a priest, I read in the documents of the church that the priest is the visible symbol or sign of unity in Christ and the bishop is the visible sign of communion. When I look back, I realize I was given a foretaste of that growing up, and it's not just a person, it is our immediate family. All of these mysterious actions of God . . . in hindsight you realize that experience was not wasted, it was part of a greater scheme."

He expressed similar thoughts more formally in the preface he wrote for the publication in the Philippines of his doctoral dissertation under the title *Episcopal Collegiality and Vatican II: The Influence of Paul VI.*[1] The preface was written in 2004 after he already had been ministering in the Philippines, teaching, working with the Federation of Asian Bishops' Conferences and, most important, experiencing being a member of the episcopal college by serving as bishop of Imus for more than two years. He wrote that being a bishop made it clearer than ever not only that he was responsible for the local church, but that he was called to represent it. "My ministry has brought me to a more profound embrace of the concerns of the diocesan community, making them the sighs and joys of my heart." In meetings of bishops in the Philippines, in Asia, or at the Vatican, he said, "I bring the diocese of Imus in my heart" to the communion of the hearts of the other local churches. "And in those moments of intense communion, I am convinced that I am not alone, our diocese is not alone. I belong to a body of brother bishops and our diocese is in communion with the whole church in faith and mission."

Bishop Tagle then added that he hoped some day to do a sequel to his dissertation, focusing on how episcopal collegiality is lived "by a bishop who is learning its hard, but comforting ways from the joys and hopes, anxieties and sorrows of men and women mirrored in the hearts of their bishops." In his ecclesiology, collegiality and communion are not simply about the pope and the world's bishops praying, thinking, and acting together, but about the people of God of all the local churches being united with one another in and through their bishops.

Just as families have expectations and can be the location of tensions, so too can a diocese with its faithful, religious and priests, and its bishop. As many bishops in many countries have experienced in the past forty years, expectations and demands can get particularly heated when what is at stake is the church's public position on issues related to politics and public policy, particularly regarding abortion, divorce, and contraception. Cardinal Tagle became archbishop of Manila as the Philippines legislature and then the supreme court were debating a reproductive health law guaranteeing universal access to contraception, sexual education, and maternal care. The cardinal, like all his brother bishops, opposed the measure. But many people believed he was not outspoken enough, because he did not lead public protest marches like some people imagined some of his predecessors would have done, and he did not threaten to excommunicate or withhold Communion from Catholic politicians who supported the law. A strong group of vocal Catholics in the Philippines demanded he make some kind of public denunciation of the politicians they themselves had elected.

That's just not his style and not his vision of what it means to be church. Sometimes, he said, bishops, especially in their official statements, "sound more like the church is the sacrament of damnation rather than the sacrament of salvation. We are supposed to continue in time the saving work of Jesus and his mercy. Jesus did not come to condemn and that's what most of us are doing. And when you are not doing it, people make you feel bad as if you are not doing what you are supposed to do. Especially if you are a bishop."

Jesuit Fr. Daniel Huang, his longtime friend, admires the cardinal's approach to social and political debates. "One of the great temptations for the Philippine church," he said, is to continue believing the church should have the kind of political influence it had in centuries past, an influence the bishops used for the good of the people, but one that does not take into account a new situation of pluralism, modernity, democracy, and widespread education. "I think that Chito, because of his exposure to other societies that are not traditionally Catholic, is aware of the need for nuance, and intellectually he knows that the Philippines is becoming a more pluralistic society, and you can't speak on the basis of power and authority alone." The cardinal, he said, also recognizes that the church has its mission and the state has its duties. "You can't expect the state to do the work of the church. So his statement at the end, when the law was passed, was very telling. He said, 'Okay, this is the law; we'll do our work: we'll form consciences.' This has always been his argument. Why should the bishops expect the state to pass laws that respect church teaching? We shouldn't expect the state to do our work. If we do our own work of forming consciences and building people up, you can have a law that makes available these means (of contraception) that you say are objectionably immoral, but Catholics won't choose them." In a pluralistic society, he said, "you work not by authority, not by fiat, but you work by influence, by reason; you present arguments, you persuade."

Listening to others and teaching through persuasion, "those are just basic orientations that I think he's convinced of," Huang said. "Those are also his pastoral instincts. But it's not that he isn't decisive. If you want to hear him getting very emotional and angry, that happens when the poor are harmed or where there is corruption or where the situation of migrants is involved. He's discerning about areas where he would be more an advocate and where he'd be more dialogical." Huang says his friend is "too intelligent to demonize or to oversimplify. Chito is someone who can see complexity. About the basics he's very clear and can speak very simply, but he is not a simple man. He is aware of ambiguity and complexity, and he can be patient with those things as well."

In fact when he was preparing for his role as one of the three presidents Pope Francis named to coordinate the sessions of the 2014 extraordinary Synod of Bishops on the Family—even though it already was clear that the content could be controversial—Cardinal Tagle said he hoped for honesty and realism, not platitudes. The extraordinary synod was designed as a first stage in the bishops' discussions, a stage in which bishops and laypeople from around the world would describe what was going on in their countries, giving the bishops a picture of "the '*status quaestionis*' in all its complexity. That gives me great hope. Let us not rush into simplifying matters into clear formulae or directives—that will come—but let us allow time, let us allow the Holy Spirit to work in us."

Faith does not come to people and it does not grow in a vacuum, but in the midst of daily life with its blessings and challenges, Tagle said. He continued,

> I am more and more convinced that the church as communion—that beautiful, biblical, theological vision, and model of the church—should be translated into living action precisely through a living communication in the process of understanding the Christian message and word of God from the messy human condition. When we look at the Bible, the history of salvation, God comes and speaks God's word not only in perfect situations; in fact, God's word arises in the midst of those messy situations, confusing situations, that require people of faith and serenity, who can remain focused on the word of God in the midst of all this confusion.

He cited as an example, "the simple maiden Mary" and the "simple carpenter Joseph," who were exposed to the very complicated situation of bringing the Savior into the world as a baby when they were not yet married. "They did not panic. They made some human decisions, but they were also open to faith and the promptings of the Holy Spirit. And, wow, lo and behold, they became participants in the unfolding of God's mysterious plan. That should be part of our '*modus vivendi*,' our way of living and operating in the church."

At Tagle's installation Mass in Manila, his homily looked at lessons from the gospel story of the disciples fishing all night without success until the risen Lord appeared and told them where to cast their nets. He said,

> This simple story teaches me valuable lessons about the mission of the church and my ministry as a bishop. First of all, the mission of the church should be wholly directed by the Lord who is always present as shepherd and guide. Human efforts should continue but unless the Lord directs the catch, we labor in vain. We know that the Lord guards his church. He keeps watch with us on those long nights of confusion and helplessness in mission. When in spite of our good intentions and efforts there are still the multitude of hungry people we cannot feed, homeless people we cannot shelter, battered women and children we cannot protect, cases of corruption and injustice that we cannot remedy, the long night of the disciples in the middle of the sea continues in us. Then we grow in compassion toward our neighbors whose lives seem to be a never-ending dark night. But in our weariness, the Lord comes.[2]

The gospel story, he continued, also teaches Jesus' disciples that they must learn to look at situations with the eyes of Jesus, the eyes of faith. "When we pray, we are transformed, we see differently. A child, especially the unborn, is no longer seen as a burden but as a gift, the youth are not a problem but a promise, women are not objects but persons, laborers are not machines but partners, the poor, the differently abled are not a nuisance but our jewels, and creation is not an object of manipulation but a sign of God's sustaining love." He also said the story of Jesus and his disciples is a good reminder for Christians.

> We need to follow the Lord in our mission not individually, but together as the disciples did. Mission is an event of the church. We will be together in failure, but we will also be

together in listening to the Spirit, in beholding God's miracles, and in hauling the nets to shore. As it was then, so it is today. The ordained, the religious, and the lay faithful, including non-Catholic Christians are called to one mission, though in various states of life and with a diversity of gifts. When we take different boats and even compete against each other to get the better portion of the catch for our own teams, we are not engaging in mission. Divisiveness and destructive competition will only help sink the boat. Let us look to the one Shepherd who gathers his sheep instead of scattering them. It is the Lord!

As the new archbishop of Manila, he publicly recognized that simply holding the title would not guarantee that he would recognize the Lord. In fact, he said, "If I am not careful this position might even blind me to the Lord and to my people." Being appointed bishop is a call to even greater humility and love, he said. Jesus asked Peter three times if he loved him. "Love makes one a true shepherd, not position. I pray that my episcopal ministry and all ministries in the church may be rooted in humble and loving discipleship. I tell myself as though it were the Lord telling me, 'Chito, do not think you have become great because of your new position. Be great rather in being a beloved and loving disciple of the Lord.' "

In an interview for this book more than two years later, Cardinal Tagle said that becoming a bishop means extra learning and often the lessons come the hard way. One thing for which he was unprepared, he said, was "facing the complexities of the financial world in the sense that as a bishop, as administrator of the goods of a diocese—ohhhh—I wish it were just as simple as money in, money out. All the financial decisions that have to be made about investments, properties and the legal aspects associated with property, labor practices, and the compliance of the church. We learned about it in moral theology, but as principles: a living wage, a family wage—all of those. But it is different when you are the one tasked with administering all those goods. That's one area that I have had to learn from the school of life itself."

As a priest he was a frequent guest on radio and television programs and, as bishop of Imus, he began a popular weekly television program commenting on the coming Sunday's Scripture readings. But dealing with journalists and their questions was another area with a steep learning curve. "I didn't have any courses in media in the seminary except film appreciation," he said. In addition to religious and ethical topics, he sometimes had to field questions about controversial actions taken or inaction by his predecessors, some of whom were already deceased. "You tell the truth, but you want to be fair to people who cannot defend themselves. And at the same time, if you don't handle it well they come back and say, 'Cover up.' They don't recognize that you may be respecting the reputation of people who are already dead, and you are trying to protect the simple faithful, their sensitivity. It is only now that there are (media) seminars for bishops and priests. But I also learned it from experience."

However, he sees his media appearances not only as defensive moves designed to protect the church or the faithful but as real opportunities for evangelization. "The world of social communications and the arts are the shapers of contemporary culture, especially among the young. The young idolize actors, actresses, and singers. If they see a priest or a bishop being able to sing some of their songs—but I choose, eh, I don't sing just any song, it must communicate values— it makes a world of difference to them. This world that has always been accused of adulterating the minds of children, of being the bearer of these negative values—if they see someone befriending that world and showing that this world can be used not only for raising funds, but for conveying deep truths and the nobility of the human spirit, I say that would be fine." Which is one reason why a quick YouTube search shows dozens of videos featuring Luis Antonio Tagle singing solos or duets of sacred hymns and pop songs.

He told a story to illustrate his point: "I was at a summer youth camp and I gave a talk. Afterward, the first question that one young person raised was 'Will you sing for us?' It wasn't even related to the topic of the talk. I said, 'Oh, please, give me questions first related to the talk and we'll see about the singing later.' So they did. Then afterward another boy said, 'When will you sing for us?' I told them I hadn't prepared anything, so I would choose a song all of us knew. I would start and they would join me." The experience of singing with those young people, Tagle said, was a matter of "hearts coming together and, without people realizing it, even the words, the lyrics become sort of a common declaration of sentiments or even belief.

"After the singing, many of the young people came up to me. Some to kiss my ring, some of them asked for autographs on their T-shirts, on their books. It took another forty-five minutes, just being with them. At first, it generated questions in my mind, 'What do they think of me? Am I being put on the same level as other singers? Am I just a celebrity? Do they see me as a bishop?' The answer came a year later at another youth camp. A boy came up to me and said, 'You know bishop, the shirt that I asked you to autograph last year is still with me. I have not washed it. Every night I fold it and put it under my pillow.'" At this point in recounting the story, the cardinal's eyes welled up with tears. The boy told him, "'I have not seen my father in years' (his father worked in the Middle East) 'but with that shirt I am sure I have a father. I belong to a family, a community.' People might think it's just singing, but no, it's a pastoral act. It isn't just bringing the presence of Gospel to the world of the arts through the presence of a bishop or priest or religious, but for all you know, the people who are participating—especially the young—their presence there speaks of a hunger or a thirst. It opened my eyes: maybe that's what it means to idolize a singer or actor, maybe they are looking for a father figure, and here is a pastor and this is a better father figure. If I can be a father figure and express that to them through words and music, and enter into their world, then why not?"

He also told this story at the Philippine Bishops' Catholic Social Media Summit. Focusing on the power of social media to evangelize, he targeted the term *friend*, especially as used on Facebook, and criticized those who take pride in collecting as many friends as possible, without recognizing how many of them—like the boy with the T-shirt—truly are looking for friends, for a community, and for a sense of belonging.

As archbishop of Manila, Tagle launched a patron of the arts program in 2013. "We stage a concert of professional artists and they are eager to participate. And we discover a lot of talent, also. The mix is crucial. We invite singers, dancers, musicians who are already known, but we also invite those who are not yet too popular. The stage we are offering them can be an opportunity to get known. And they love it."

At the first concert, he said, "there was a husband and wife, singers who used to sing on London's West End and on Broadway, then they came back to the Philippines and now their singing career as a couple is flourishing. But last year, backstage waiting for their turn, I was there and they just opened their hearts, and I learned the woman had cancer. The woman said, 'I don't know how long I will live. If this is my last performance, then let it be for God.' These are artists. And the husband said, 'I hope this will not be our last performance together, but I will give it my best.' " Once again, the cardinal's eyes filled with tears as he talked about the touching encounter.

The patron of the arts concert always ends with the archbishop singing. "I know I cannot match the quality" of the professionals' singing performance, but, he said, the people are appreciative. The proceeds from the concert go to a specific charity each year, and those who buy tickets know that. "So this is also missionary; the last concert we had was to support a housing project for the poor. So, I say to the people after my song, 'The need is great to help these poor people, so I have to stretch myself and sing for the sake of the poor.' " The reaction, he says, "makes you humble."

There is one more thing the cardinal said the seminary never prepared him for, something that came as quite a shock. "Of course, the church is also a human institution, so there is what some would call 'church politics.' And there is no course in the seminary preparing you for that. I refuse to be political in the pejorative sense. When I was teaching ecclesiology I always taught my students that the only politics allowed in church is communion, not power struggle. That is not church, that is not how I perceive Christ the head, so why should the body be different. The politics is that of communion." When church members seem focused on power rather than unity, "it gives me sadness and worries me and wearies me. I get tired when I am pushed into that area. Sometimes when my confreres notice, they say why were you quiet? Why did you not utter a word? They notice it. Of course, I cannot say plainly, 'I don't want to engage in that heavy political talk where everyone is grandstanding, just trying to impress other people and gain points before the Holy Father.' "

Now that the former Cardinal Jorge Mario Bergoglio of Buenos Aires is pope, Cardinal Tagle laughs sheepishly about one area in which he definitely didn't make points with the pope. He and Bergoglio were among the main speakers at the 2008 International Eucharistic Congress in Quebec, and they already knew each other from serving together on the general council of the Synod of Bishops. "I think three times he wrote to me when I was in my first Diocese of Imus. Unfortunately, I don't remember responding to any of his letters."

"We were on very friendly terms," he said. "In between the meetings of the (synod) council, we would discuss things," and over the years "he would give remarks to me, comments about an interview with me that he had read. And after my talk in Quebec, he was one of the first to approach me and say, 'What a wonderful catechesis.' He was very encouraging."

In an interview about a year after Pope Francis's election, Cardinal Tagle said,

[The year] has been a celebration of the many things Cardinal Bergoglio and I hold in common. For me, it's a deeply personal joy. His first year in a way articulated many of the things that I believed in and probably could not or have not been able to articulate verbally or even pastorally in terms of action. At the same time, many of the things that he has said or taught so far have also affirmed some of the things I have said and done, and which probably were not understood by some or not fully appreciated by some. It has really given me a lot of joy, a joy that strengthens. You know, once in a while I also entertain doubts: 'Is that insight of mine really good? Am I just being adventurous?' But then you have someone like him, and I get this confirmation, this affirmation of some things.

Father Joseph Komonchak, who directed Tagle's doctoral dissertation at The Catholic University of America in Washington, DC, said, "He was, in many respects by the way he exercised his ministry, a Pope Francis before Pope Francis. He lived a very simple life. He never owned an automobile. He would take public transportation—and if you've ever been to Manila, you know that's a challenge—from where he lived to the seminary and to the Ateneo. He's very, very committed to the poor; it's been part of his own preaching and style of life right from the beginning."

Cardinal Tagle said he sees Pope Francis embracing "a more evangelical, Gospel style of being and style of leading, which makes us in a way self-critical of what we have inherited and wanting to purify those things in the light of the Gospel. For me it's a welcome development. I know many, many sectors in the society and in the Philippine church are very happy with that. But at the same time, that makes the church, especially the leaders, open and vulnerable to critique, and I guess it's a call to humility again. We have gotten used to ways of doing things and ways of thinking that have become second nature, so having these moments where we are being pricked by his words, by his testimony and witness, and also by the questions being raised by critical voices—they bring a little pain, but I guess it's also pain that liberates. You just have to be open."

Four months before Pope Benedict XVI resigned he convoked a Synod of Bishops to discuss evangelization. The induction of Tagle into the College of Cardinals was announced during the synod. And, as it turns out, Cardinal

Tagle believes Pope Francis is shaping what Tagle had told the synod the church needed to be in order to evangelize effectively. The cardinal described it as "a church that is more humble, a church that listens, a church that doesn't pretend to have all the answers, a church that can be as confused as other people in the disorder of their lives, a church that is reduced to silence—the silence of someone who contemplates, not the silence of someone who is angry."

Cardinal Tagle said he has been promoting and trying to live those attitudes for years. He said that especially in the midst of the Philippine debate over the reproductive health bill, "some people have been critical of me for not being the angry prophet, condemning people left and right, those who do not support the official position of the church. But my silence is not because I do not care, but the silence of someone who knows a lot of the mess of the human condition and dilemmas that people go through, the difficulty of finding solutions. For me, sometimes, the most effective response the church can give to those people is a silent presence that assures that we may not agree with everything you have done with your life, but we are here to share the pain and sorrow you are experiencing."

CHAPTER FIVE

Shaped by Vatican II

"What do you say about the revolution of Pope Francis?"

It's a question Cardinal Tagle has been asked frequently. He said he has a ready answer: "Revolution? He calls the church to get out of itself. I say, 'That's not Pope Francis, that's Vatican II.' The pope is just leading us back to the church at Vatican II. So when we say the pope is teaching us something new, it's a sign that we have not received Vatican II. And he's telling us, 'Rediscover Vatican II and receive it, *por favor*.'"

Marking the fiftieth anniversary of the promulgation of *Lumen Gentium*, the Second Vatican Council's constitution on the church, Cardinal Tagle gave several talks in Rome in late November 2014. Like Pope Francis, he does not question the value of the council, nor does he enter into the recent polemics about its interpretation. In his view, the council was the work of the church under the guidance of the Holy Spirit and the leadership first of St. John XXIII then of Blessed Paul VI. Catholics today have an obligation to study its documents and continually discern how best to respond to its main messages: the universal call to holiness and the need for the Catholic community to be outgoing, to reach out and not spend the best of its energy focusing on itself.

Lumen Gentium, especially its first chapter, led to a renewed self-understanding of the church, especially in Asia, the cardinal said.

> [*Lumen Gentium*] describes a church that is other-centered, a church that is not self-focused. The church exists for the kingdom of God and the church exists for the world. The church does not exist for itself. [The life and mission of the church] is totally dedicated to Jesus, the kingdom, and to the world—Jesus, whose light the church must shed on the world. The church is able to serve the world precisely because of its relationship with Jesus Christ, a relationship that makes the church a kind of sacrament, a sign and instrument, of intimate communion with God and unity among human beings. [The church isn't being pulled in two directions.] It is not either/or: more of Christ and less of the world or more of the world and less of Christ. No. The very life of the church is being other-centered: Jesus and the world. Shedding the light of Christ on the world and bringing the world to the light of Christ.[1]

The inspiration for the "other-centeredness of the church" is the life of the Trinity, Cardinal Tagle continued,

> the Father creating the world, creating humankind in order to share divine life. And when humanity failed, God continued going out of God's self by sending the Son, who went out of himself, became human, died for all of us. The first fruit of the resurrection—the Holy Spirit—is sent to re-create the world. We have a God who is not focused on himself.
>
> The church as the icon of the Trinity cannot be other than other-centered like God. You cannot say, "Oh, the present pope wants us to go out and then another will say, come

in." Go out. Come in. Go out. No. Our God is an extrovert God, always getting out of God's self, saving, and most dramatically with the incarnation, getting out. This is the mystery of the church.

The process of "reception" or receiving the teaching of the Second Vatican Council in North America was marked, in some quarters, by what have been called "liturgical wars," debates over the extent of reform called for by the Second Vatican Council and over the latitude individual priests and bishops' conferences should have in translating the Mass texts and adding or changing gestures. Later, a debate that began in Europe spread to North America as well, a debate focused on differences over the interpretation of the council as a whole. Some theologians and commentators have accused others, including Cardinal Tagle because of his scholarly work, of putting an excessive emphasis on Vatican II's calls for reform, so much so that the council could be seen as marking a "rupture" with tradition. Others have been criticized for such an excessive emphasis on "continuity" that any change in church practice, no matter how minor, would appear to go against the council's true wishes.

When Archbishop Tagle's nomination to the College of Cardinals was announced in 2012, and again when he entered the conclave in 2013 to elect Pope Benedict's successor (and some hailed him as a potential papal candidate), commentators belonging to the "continuity" bloc raised alarms about the work Fr. Tagle did from 1995 to 2001 as a member of the Institute for Religious Sciences in Bologna, Italy, and his contribution to the institute's magnum opus, the five-volume *History of Vatican II*. The English edition of the work, published in 2006, was coedited by Giuseppe Alberigo and Fr. Joseph Komonchak, Tagle's doctoral director.

Archbishop Agostino Marchetto, a former secretary of the Pontifical Council for Migrants and Itinerant People, was seen as a leading proponent of those who insisted Vatican II had to be read in continuity with the past. He criticized those who looked for all the ways it charted a new course. He and other critics believed such an interpretation left the Vatican II documents without a firm foundation and led many people to the mistaken impression that the so-called "Spirit of Vatican II" meant allowing almost anything. As successive volumes of *History of Vatican II* were published, Marchetto wrote scathing reviews. In 2005 the Vatican publishing house released a collection of his reviews; the English translation of this volume is titled *The Second Vatican Ecumenical Council: A Counterpoint for the History of the Council.* It includes a critique of Tagle's chapter in the history, "The 'Black Week' of Vatican II (November 14–21, 1964)." The term "Black Week" has been attributed to a Dutch bishop participating in Vatican II, but it was picked up by the media and became a fairly common way of referring to that week of the council's third session. Some bishops at the council were upset that week by unexpected delays and additions: the announcement that the decree on religious liberty would not be voted upon until the next year; Pope Paul VI's revisions to the decree on ecumenism; the pope's explanatory note on collegiality to accompany *Lumen Gentium*; and the pope's proclamation of Mary as "Mother of the Church" although many bishops felt that the declaration of new Marian titles would be seen as anti-ecumenical by other Christians.

Marchetto took issue, first of all, with Tagle's use of the phrase Black Week, saying it was journalistic, not objective and not scholarly, even though by the time the history was written it had entered common parlance. "The abundance of funereal 'color' within the tempestuous framework" described by Tagle, he said, "provides a good indication of the interpretive direction favored by this author." However, Marchetto wrote, "it is a rather rich and even profound study in some ways."

Writing his chapter for *The History of Vatican II* thirty years after Vatican II closed, Tagle, who had written his doctoral dissertation on "Episcopal Collegiality in the Teaching and Practice of Paul VI," said many of the initial reactions in the so-called Black Week "were prompted by the impressions of the moment and are not sustainable now that the complexity of the situations is better known." Part of that complexity, he said, "was that its tone depended on who was narrating the story, who was listening, and when and where the story was told."[2] From his perspective, the delayed vote on the religious freedom document allowed improvements to the text; the changes to the decree on ecumenism proved to have little significance and did not stop the Catholic Church from making huge strides in its commitment to dialogue for the restoration of Christian unity; the note on collegiality did not put an end to the question—which continues to be debated—about the relationship between the bishops and the pope; and the proclamation of Mary as Mother of the Church appears to have had little impact on the church's relations with its ecumenical partners.

Marchetto is a fierce critic, not just of *The History of Vatican II* but of its main editor, Alberigo, and anyone associated with his institute, the "Bologna School." Marchetto has claimed the Bologna School had the money and the influence to "monopolize" interpretations of the council, presenting it as a revolutionary break with the past that promoted democracy and participation in the church, almost excluding the role of the hierarchy in protecting and promoting the truths of faith. The archbishop also has insisted that a serious history of Vatican II would need to rely more on the official acts and documents of the council and less on the diaries and correspondence of participants. Komonchak, who coedited the English edition of the history and wrote several of its chapters said, "Marchetto's book is not a counterweight in the sense of being another history of the council; it is a series of book reviews. He is not proposing an alternate history. I went back and reread what he had to say about Tagle's chapter in Volume IV. He said it was *'uno studio ricco e approfondito'*—well-researched or well-investigated—and he says he regrets the use of the journalistic language," particularly the phrase Black Week. Komonchak said that instead of addressing Tagle's presentation point by point, Marchetto picked out passages that, in his view, lack objectivity or present questionable hypotheses. "Then he proceeds simply to cite a series of citations from various pages, with phrases and clauses taken out of context, with no arguments to indicate why Marchetto thinks them incorrect or lacking. It's not a serious piece of criticism," Komonchak concluded.

Even more, the retired professor insists that the idea that a Bologna School exists is "simply a myth." Dozens of theologians and historians from around the world contributed to the five volumes and their work represents a wide variety of approaches and emphases. Komonchak said he did two major pieces for the history "and I was never expected to follow some kind of party line and no changes were made in my presentation." In the mid-1980s, when the volumes were being planned, "the atmosphere—the context of studies of Vatican II—was much less fraught than it became later. We set out to do a serious history of the council. And my own research was heavily into that. I simply took the council for granted. This culture war in regard to the council simply wasn't burning then. I set out to do what needed to be done."

Father Chito's decision "to do a dissertation on Paul VI and collegiality had nothing to do with these kinds of hermeneutical disputes about Vatican II," Komonchak said in an interview from Bloomingburg, NY, where he lives in retirement. Tagle "simply sat down to do a serious piece of work and then he went and worked in both Bologna and in Brescia (Italy) at the Paul VI archives, so he did a lot of original research on the matter. If anything, I would say his interest in Paul VI would set him apart from the Alberigo approach to the council, which focused so powerfully and sometimes even exclusively on John XXIII."

Chito was just eight years old when the council ended and was in the seminary when its liturgical changes and adaptation to local cultures began to blossom. "He's enthusiastic about the council, and I'm sure he regards it as a source of great grace for the whole church," Komonchak said. "I think that's how his chapter in *The History of Vatican II* ends, and he's trying to live the ecclesiology of the council himself. He grew up in the church as it was transformed by Vatican II and just takes it for granted, I think."

Father Tagle's chapter ends: "Without the Black Week, Vatican II would not have been the council it ended up being. From it sprang wonderful lessons, beautiful documents, exciting horizons, and painful wounds as well. Ultimately, the forces of renewal unleashed by Vatican II were so powerful that the incidents of the Black Week could not hinder them. Indeed the Black Week was one of the wellsprings that have made the Second Vatican Council a source of grace for the church and for the world."[3]

In his talks about *Lumen Gentium* on the occasion of the document's fiftieth anniversary, Cardinal Tagle was asked to focus particularly on its reception and impact on the church in Asia. He zeroed in on the document's explanation of the church's relationship to the world.

> *Lumen Gentium* recognizes that the world comes from God and the world was assumed by Jesus in his incarnation, and the Holy Spirit continues to blow mightily on this world. So the church fosters and even takes to itself the capacities, the resources and customs of people insofar as they are good. The church purifies, strengthens and ennobles them. In return, the gifts of the people contribute to the good of the church. This is what we call "concrete catholicity." The church is not afraid of the world. Because the Son of God assumed the world, became part of it, the church gets out of itself, inhabits the world and allows the world to influence it.
>
> The "concrete catholicity" of the church, according to *Lumen Gentium*, is both an instrument and a fruit of the church's orientation and service to the world and humanity. The Catholic unity of diverse peoples and cultures is not self-serving for the church, rather it witnesses to universal peace, the universal peace that the kingdom of God promises. [The Vatican II statement also means] we are not here to conquer the world, but to serve the world—it's a very humble vision of the world.[4]

In receiving, interpreting, and applying the teachings of the Second Vatican Council, the bishops of Asia—through the Federation of Asian Bishops' Conferences, which was founded in the early 1970s—began by "looking at the faces of Asia," its diverse peoples, their gifts and challenges, their ancient religions and cultures. They looked, Tagle said, and they heard the people of Asia calling, "Come and serve us."

Being Christian always means imitating Christ, Tagle explained, so the bishops began to study the best ways they could respond like Jesus to the hopes and needs of the people of Asia, bringing Jesus and his Gospel to the people out of a conviction that he is the answer to people's deepest aspirations. "No reception of Vatican II will happen in our backyards without looking at the world, seeing the light of Christ as the answer, and then going through this process of commitment to renewal, gratitude (grateful memory), repentance, and commitment."

While North Americans and Europeans seemed concerned primarily over the liturgical changes in the wake of Vatican II, when it came to Asia the concern was over the balance between dialogue and proclamation. Cardinal Tagle said there was no "war" over the topic within the Catholic Church in Asia, but "some people in the Vatican" raised questions. They saw the Asian bishops' focus on dialogue as being a total negation of evangelization. Debate over how dialogue and proclamation of the Gospel could go hand in hand lasted for decades. In 1991 the Pontifical Council for Interreligious Dialogue published guidelines under the title "Dialogue and Proclamation," calling for balance between dialogue and evangelization. Proclaiming Christ, it said, must be done with sensitivity, humility, and respect for other cultures, and that requires knowledge of the other and dialogue. It also means that bishops and ordinary Catholics in any given place will need to inculturate their dialogue and proclamation, just as they inculturate their piety and prayer.

Tagle explained,

> The bishops of Asia realized that preaching the Gospel in Asia demanded their Asian brand of receiving *Lumen Gentium*. Preaching the Gospel in Asia demanded that the life and teaching of Christ must be made incarnate in the minds and lives of our people. Vatican II used the language of relationship: the church is related to the world, the church

is related to our non-Catholic or non-Christian brothers and sisters. But the church in Asia went beyond the language of relationship. They (the bishops) opted for the language of incarnation, the mystery of incarnation, the going out, the kenosis, the self-emptying of Jesus to be united with humanity. The fruit of this Christ-like immersion in the human condition is a truly local church. There! Look at the reception: The realization and enfleshment of the body of Christ in a given people, a given place and time.

In a region of the world where Christians make up only about 7 percent of the population, Cardinal Tagle said, "for the church to be incarnate in the peoples of Asia, the manner of service, the manner of evangelization takes the form of dialogue . . . a humble, loving dialogue." Working in the Federation of Asian Bishops' Conferences, the bishops have focused on dialogue in three areas: with cultures, with religions, and with the poor. "Whatever truly belongs to the people—meanings and values, aspirations, thoughts, languages, songs and artistry, even frailties and failings—the church in Asia will dialogue with them," the cardinal said. Huge numbers of Asian people are "poor materially, but rich in human values, qualities and potential," he continued. Once again emphasizing the need for the church to listen, he said that "the dialogue of life with the poor is not at all paternalistic. It demands, according to the bishops of Asia, 'working with them, learning from them, enabling them to identify and articulate their aspirations' leading to a genuine commitment on the part of the church to bring about social justice in Asian societies in accordance with the spirit and demands of the Gospel."

Another part of the dialogue with the peoples of Asia, he said, is dialogue with what the Asian bishops described in

1974 as the "church of silence"—at that time presumably the Catholics in Vietnam and China living under religious restrictions and oppression. "Dialoguing with those who are not allowed to speak" calls for further local adaptation, it means engaging in "a dialogue of solidarity, of witnessing, of prayer and of remembrance at the Eucharistic banquet— a very powerful way of dialoguing with the church of silence," the cardinal said.

The silence of those who have been officially silenced is "not the empty kind of silence, but the silently loud witness of a faith that faces death for the Beloved," he continued. "The church of Asia continues to dialogue with the martyrs who were silenced. The church in Asia grows and appropriates its true identity over and over again through dialogue with the martyrs. Many of these martyrs are nameless. That's why they could not be officially beatified and canonized. Imagine the church of the silent and the nameless who died uttering the name of Jesus. And now they continue in silence to utter that name, the name of the Word of God who became flesh on Asian soil."

Despite centuries of missionary activity that brought people not only the Gospel, but also European philosophy, theology, and piety, the Asian bishops after the Second Vatican Council laid claim to the truth that "Jesus was born on Asian soil." The cardinal said, "He became incarnate there so the church would follow him, incarnate in people's cultures, histories, and traditions, even in their silence." A truly local church, he said, "arises from the intersection of the Gospel and the people in their concrete cultures, religious traditions and situations of poverty."

Cardinal Tagle obviously is aware of Marchetto's negative appraisal of his work in *The History of Vatican II* and of similar criticisms in the writings of the well-known Italian pundit and journalist, Sandro Magister. But for the cardinal, that too is part of the naturally long process of reception of a council's teaching. Speaking at Rome's Centro Pro Unione in November 2014, Tagle used the definition of "reception" formulated by International Theological Commission, an advisory body to the Congregation for the Doctrine of the Faith. (The cardinal himself was a member of the commission as a young priest when it was headed by Cardinal Joseph Ratzinger, the future Pope Benedict XVI.) The commission defined reception as "as a process by which, guided by the Spirit, the people of God recognizes intuitions or insights and integrates them into the patterns and structures of its life and worship, accepting a new witness to the truth and corresponding forms of its expression, because it perceives them to be in accord with the apostolic Tradition."[5]

The cardinal also emphasized a point made by the German theologian Hermann Pottmeyer that the process of reception includes a process of interpretation as well.

> When we receive the teaching of Vatican II we interpret, and of course in the interpretation we bring out our own temperaments, our own histories, our own experiences—they all contribute to our understanding and interpretation of Vatican II. The reception, the assimilation by so vast an ecclesial community requires time, time for rethinking, time for conversion, time for developing a new self-understanding. With that process we have to expect different interpretations of a doctrine that is being received. It is normal for diverging, contradictory interpretations to be part of the whole process of reception. Let us not be afraid when opinions differ. They are part of the process. They are part of the interpretation. And through the Holy Spirit, things will level off, without

removing diversity in the understanding and interpretation of a teaching.

The exercise of collegiality is one of the areas that continues to be explored, debated, and tested in the church. As Cardinal Tagle tries to ensure communion and collegiality in his own archdiocese, with the other bishops of the Philippines, and with the bishops of the Federation of Asian Bishops' Conferences, he says he often looks to Blessed Paul VI. "I remember one of his rules in life as the presider over the Second Vatican Council, as the implementer: 'No one defeated; everyone convinced,'" the cardinal said in an interview with Catholic News Service. "He would take the extra step, go the extra mile, to convince people who find difficulties with this or that. And in the process he would be attacked from all sides. In doing my research, I was able to read some of the letters he got from cardinals, the bishops from different sectors of the church. I could just imagine the depth of suffering and also the depth of spirituality of this man, who would never become popular, who would never become a star the way the other popes were."[6]

Speaking more specifically about collegiality, the cardinal said, "I really admire Pope Paul VI for keeping the balance, in the sense of fidelity to the biblical data: Jesus called the Twelve as twelve. While he called them by name, he also constituted them as a body. And he entrusted his mission to them together, as a body. So the communion that is the church is supposed to be lived on the ministerial level among the bishops. It has to be expressed in concrete forms and one of those forms is the Synod of Bishops."

Cardinal Tagle is more familiar with the synodal form than most bishops his age. He has been attending synods at the Vatican since 1998, when he served as an expert at the special Synod of Bishops for Asia. Later, as bishop of Imus, his brother bishops of the Philippines elected him to the 2008 synod on the Bible; and the bishops at that gathering elected Bishop Tagle to the general council of the synod, the body that helps the pope prepare his post-synodal apostolic exhortation and prepares the *lineamenta* or outline for the next general synod. Pope Benedict XVI appointed him to the 2012 synod on new evangelization and announced Tagle's induction into the College of Cardinals as the synod was meeting. Pope Francis named him one of the three presidents of the 2014 extraordinary synod on the family and one of four presidents for the 2015 general synod, also on the family.

In church leadership and governance, Tagle said, there has always been a "dynamic tension" between the primacy of the pope and collegiality because

> the body of bishops only exists with the Holy Father, who is bishop of Rome and therefore the primate, the pastor. While he exercises primacy, he is never divorced from the church and the body. That debate has always been present in the synod. There came a time when, according to those who participated in many synods, the synodal process leaned more toward the primacy rather than the participation of the bishops. So the bishops deliberated, but then it was the pope who issued a statement in his own name, though the post-synodal apostolic exhortation reflects the discussions. . . . Now there seems to be a re-appreciation of the dynamic tension in the whole synodal process.[7]

He said he was happy the 2014 extraordinary synod on the family concluded with the beatification of Pope Paul VI, "the one who instituted the Synod of Bishops and who, in a way, saved the collegial process by being true to the doctrine, but opening it to what some people might call compromise, but compromise is not always bad. Compromise sometimes allows those who have difficulties to receive the doctrine."

In his chapter on the Black Week in *History of Vatican II*, the future cardinal wrote, "Whenever the 'Black Week' is remembered, the figure of Paul VI almost automatically enters as a villain, as someone who sided with the belligerent minority or at least allowed it to prevail" as the council's third session was drawing to a close in 1964. As for Pope Paul's decision to send "authoritative" support for delaying the vote on the declaration on religious liberty, he wrote that it was motivated by "the desire to save the council's whole project" on the theme, and the fact "that it happened in the middle of a stormy week made it appear worse than it actually was." On another of the events that week, he said the pope's explanatory note on *Lumen Gentium* was "meant to clarify the relationship between the pope and the members of the episcopal college." He used the word *ironic* to describe the fact that Pope Paul's "efforts to illuminate the thorny issue were conducted in the bitter atmosphere of a collegial act: the celebration of an ecumenical council." He said the note was the pope's attempt to preserve the direction the majority of bishops at Vatican II were going without losing all the votes of those who feared it could be interpreted as overturning the First Vatican Council's teaching on the primacy of the pope. At the same time, he said, the note could have been aimed at "both the minority who feared the doctrine and the majority who went beyond what the doctrine stated."[8] The note insisted the head of the college of bishops—the pope—and the members were not equal; that one becomes and remains a member of the college through both consecration and communion with the pope and other members of the college; and that the power of the college exists only when it is united with the head.

Speaking about Paul VI on the eve of his beatification, Cardinal Tagle said he admires him for his dedication to the renewal of the church and for his great humility. In the pope's last testament, the cardinal points out, he said, "No monument for me," so he is buried in the ground in the grotto under St. Peter's Basilica with a simple marble slab on top. Whenever in Rome, "I always go there" to pray, the cardinal said.

CHAPTER SIX

Lessons of Listening

Cardinal Tagle knows how to work a crowd. Even while studying for his doctorate at The Catholic University in Washington, he was in demand as a preacher and speaker. As the years have passed, he has gone from small venues to cathedrals and stadiums, tapping into Catholics' longing for a deeper faith life, for forms of devotion that nourish their family and societal relationships, and for church leaders who truly seem to understand the realities and challenges of their lives. The same gifts that make him popular with lay Catholics also have caught the notice of popes and Vatican officials, who have given him key roles at international Eucharistic Congresses and at the Synod of Bishops.

Whether in a press conference, at a fundraising concert, or in the Vatican Synod Hall, he demonstrates impeccable timing as he lets his audience laugh at his foibles, then gives them enough of a nudge that they see a similar need for mercy or a similar longing for wholeness and coherence in their own lives. Tears come easily to his eyes and people believe him because he is moved by the stories of pain he shares. His smile is mischievous, his jokes catch people by surprise, and his dreams for a more just world are relayed with such passion that people get caught up in his dreaming and begin to feel that they, too, can be part of making it come true.

The Sunday before Pope Francis arrived in the Philippines in January 2015, Cardinal Tagle had two important Masses on his schedule: the first followed a ground-breaking cere- mony for homes for people who had been living in shacks along a polluted and flood-prone creek. The second was at the Church of the Santo Niño in Tondo on the outskirts of Manila where thousands gathered as part of a novena to the Child Jesus. It was the feast of the Baptism of the Lord and Cardinal Tagle gave basically the same homily in both locations, focusing on baptism as the mandate moment for Jesus' public ministry and as the source of each Christian's call to go forth and share the Gospel. He went through each age group, telling children to share God's love at school and at play. But he really showed how he watches and listens when he told preteens their mission was not about texting as fast as they could to as many friends as they could find. (His miming text messaging reflected his own speed at using his cellphone.) And the congregations roared when, refer- encing specific Philippine TV commercials, he told teenagers and young adults their purpose in life was not to try out as many products as humanly possible to clear up acne. They laughed when he listed a variety of popular skin care brands and pretended to frantically follow the traditional Philippine solution of pressing papaya against each pimple. Asked later how he knew so much about skin care trends, he said it was impossible to turn on the television without seeing the ads.

As the cardinal arrived and departed both Masses, the crowds pressed around him, reminiscent of how people reach for the pope. Patiently he allowed people to take his hand and press it to their foreheads, which is the traditional Philippine sign of respect. But when elderly men or women did it, he always took their hands next and pressed them to his own forehead.

At a book presentation in Manila in 2004, his longtime friend Jesuit Fr. Daniel Huang introduced Tagle with a reflection on why he has so many fans. First, Huang said, it is because he "is a theologian of striking, original, profound insight. When you hear him speak, you always see your faith and your life in a new way. He has a magnificent way of explaining things with such clarity and simplicity, and yet with such depth." Furthermore, Huang continued, he "brings us joy. Have you ever been bored by a talk by Chito?" And then, he said, there's the passion. "When he speaks, you know there is a fire within, a burning desire, a holy obsession for a new social order and a renewed church where the poor are welcomed, where women are honored, where the other is accepted, where there is no more discrimination and violence, but only compassion and peace."

In both the witty and the wise, Cardinal Tagle's talks reflect his personal experience; his words ring with the authenticity of one who has listened to others and who really tries to practice what he preaches. As Huang said, "What he speaks about, he lives in his life of service, humility, simplicity of life, prophecy and shepherding God's people."

The International Eucharistic Congress talk—the one that Tagle said received a thumbs-up from the future Pope Francis —started off slowly with a somewhat complicated vision of where Tagle said he was taking it. But, as a good speaker, he knew it was hard going for his audience. So he grabbed their attention and got them back on board with a well-placed "Are you with me?" Then he started preaching with a style that could rival many televangelists. His topic at the 2008 congress in Quebec was "The Eucharist, the Life of Christ in Our Lives: Spiritual Worship and Authentic Adoration."

His key point was that "because the life of Christ is oriented toward others, the church must share this life with the world. The life of Christ is his gift to the church that is meant to be the church's gift to the world." Tagle looked at what made Jesus' worship of God and the sacrifice he offered different from what anyone else had ever offered God in prayer: "the surrender of his humanity."[1]

Jesus' obedience to God and "his solidarity with feeble sinners" make his sacrifice an act of worship, Tagle said. "His oneness with weak humanity was essential to his priestly service or worship on behalf of the people." What is more, "his embrace of the trials and sufferings of human beings has made him a brother who can now truly intercede for them before the Father's mercy rather than judge them harshly." In every celebration of the Eucharist, Jesus renews that sacrifice and invites us to share in his self-giving worship.

Bishop Tagle's talk gained steam as he noted,

> quite often, Jesus was denounced as a violator of God's law when he showed compassion for the weak, the poor, the sick, the women, and public sinners. He offered new life to those considered impure by eating and mingling with them. He assured them that God was not distant and there was hope in God's loving mercy. But he himself got no mercy from his adversaries, only ridicule for disobeying laws that were supposed to embody God's will. Jesus suffered on account of his self-offering for those loved by God. But he never wavered in his sacrifice. In the process he exposed the false gods that people worshiped, erroneous notions of holiness and the blindness of righteous people to the visitations of God. Jesus' sacrifice uncovered the link

between the worship of false gods and insensitivity to the
needy. An idolater easily loses compassion for the weak.

The church that lives the life of Christ and offers his living
sacrifice cannot run away from its mission to unearth the
false gods worshiped by the world. How many people have
exchanged the true God for idols like profit, prestige, plea-
sure and control? [Yet] we cannot just point to others, we
should examine ourselves. Like those who opposed Jesus
in the name of authentic religion, we could be blind to God
and neighbors because of self-righteousness, spiritual pride
and rigidity of mind. Ecclesiastical customs and persons,
when naively and narrowly deified and glorified, might
become hindrances to true worship and compassion. I am
disturbed when some people who do not even know me
personally conclude that my being a bishop automatically
makes me closer to God than they could ever be, [explain-
ing they seem to think] my words are God's words, my
desires are God's, my anger is God's, and my actions are
God's—oh my, what power! If I am not cautious, I might
just believe it and start demanding the offerings of the best
food and wine, money, car, house, adulation, and submis-
sion. After all, I am God! I might take so much delight in
my stature and its benefits that I might end up being in-
sensitive to the needs of the poor and the earth.[2]

Tagle went on to talk about Eucharistic adoration and
how, if it is a true act of adoration of Jesus' sacrifice, it must
lead to prayers not just for oneself but particularly for the
world's most defenseless and vulnerable people.

When we adore the Triune God in praise of the sacrifice
of Jesus, we are called to cry for the victims of the indif-
ference of sinful humanity and the helplessness of God.
But we also cry in gratitude for the hopeful unfolding of
pure love in a broken world. I wish that Eucharistic adora-

tion would lead us to know Jesus more as the compassionate companion of many crucified peoples of today. Let us spend time too with the multitudes of innocent victims of our time. We might be able to touch Jesus who knows their tears and pain for he has made them his own and has changed them into hope and love.[3]

The Vatican tapped him again for the speakers' list at the International Eucharistic Congress in Dublin in 2012. His main talk was titled, "Communion in the Word through Mary," and was a meditation on the meaning of communion, of being brothers and sisters with each other, and on the attitudes of Mary the church must mirror to the world. Those attitudes include: "not advancing its own projects, but the will of God"; being a companion of the poor; listening to the lowly "with reverential silence (and) listening to God speaking through them"; looking "for Jesus among the lost, wounded, tired and abandoned" and leading them to the Father's house; and being "attentive to the emptiness experienced by our age" and leading people "not to us, but to Jesus for he alone can make miracles happen."

"Jesus tells us to take care of the sorrowful mothers and fathers, for they are our parents, too," he told the people gathered in Dublin. "He tells us to look after the lost children of the world, for they are our sons and daughters, too. No wound is so great that it could not be healed by love. By being in communion with the Word, the church, like Mary, will be the seed of the new family of justice, healing and peace."[4]

Holding the congress in Ireland, a land whose traditional Catholic faith was shaken to the core by the clerical sexual abuse crisis, organizers insisted discussions about the crisis and the need for healing and justice, particularly for victims, be part of the program. Tagle gave a workshop at the congress titled, "The Abuse of Children: Accepting Responsibility,

Bringing Justice." The cardinal repeated many of the points he made four months earlier at a Vatican-sponsored conference on preventing abuse for bishops and religious superiors from around the world.

In the Dublin talk, like at the Vatican conference, Tagle acknowledged that while some church people still considered clerical sexual abuse to be a problem only in Anglo-Saxon countries, he was convinced the bishops of Asia needed to be honest and vigilant, recognizing that while very few cases made the news or were brought before the courts, "to pretend that no problem exists does not help at all."

He told the Dublin audience that he came not as an expert in the problem of abuse, "but as someone who searches with you, searches with my fellow bishops, searches with the many victims who are still looking for answers and I am with you also as someone who hopes for healing and for a way for us to still be able to work and walk together." In the Philippines, he said, that means bishops must be attentive to cultural attitudes and practices that may make it easier for abuse to occur and harder to detect: power and respect automatically conferred on elders and people in positions of authority, including priests; a culture that is comfortable with frequent touching; a culture in which the abused feel shame and believe that shame reflects on their whole families; a culture that regards the clergy as "more than ordinary human beings," he said.

The clerical sexual abuse crisis should challenge the church to deepen its understanding of celibacy, which is a practice valued in Asian societies and among Asia's traditional religions. However, Tagle said, "many people think that celibacy is simply a rule the conservative church has to observe for the sake of tradition, but it is not that. Some make it the culprit for all types of sexual misconduct as though removing celibacy automatically removes sexual misconduct. Others defend it, but in a narrowly legalistic way that proves ineffectual." The cardinal said the Catholic Church needs "a serene, but comprehensive consideration of the matter: Is it negative—I don't have a wife—or is it truly an expression of pastoral charity?"

Every bishop and every diocese should have a pastoral plan in place to promote healing and justice when abuse occurs, Tagle said. "The first element of a response is the pastoral care of the victims and their families. Pastoral care encompasses justice for them, compassion for them, protection for them, and even restitution in some cases." The cardinal said that while it is "painful to listen to victims," allowing them to tell their stories can help their process of healing and "hopefully awakens compassion in us." In addition, "we learn the dynamics of victimization and the victim's reaction to their situation," which in turn helps the church understand what to look for and what victims really need.

The cardinal also insisted on pastoral care for the parish where an accused priest ministered. The priest is removed, the victim can change residence or change parishes, but the community remains. "The Asian propensity to quickly restore 'harmony' often makes us believe that healing has already occurred when it really has not," he said.

Cardinal Tagle said bishops and religious superiors also need support when they find out one of their priests has abused someone. "It is difficult and painful to be a superior or a bishop nowadays. They feel lost when a cleric commits sexual abuse. As they help their priests, they also have to judge on a matter many of them do not fully grasp," he said. "At the same time, they cannot defend the priest while neglecting truth, justice and the good of the victims and their community."

"Superiors feel battered from all sides," he said. "They are accused of covering up if they try to be discreet. If they are firm, they are accused of a lack of compassion."

Cardinal Tagle's clear, simple, and unusual way of speaking even in the most formal settings already garnered the attention of the media and top church leaders from around the world at the 2005 world Synod of Bishops on the Eucharist, the 2008 Synod of Bishops on the Bible, and the 2012 synod on new evangelization. In each synod, most of the bishops' speeches fell into one of two categories: describing the situation in their home country—often lamenting a lack of solid Catholic education and/or cultural forces leading the faithful astray—or providing a "showcase" for the bishop's theological expertise on the topic. Unlike them, Tagle disarmed people.

At the synod on the Eucharist in 2005, he spoke about the shortage of priests in the Philippines and the faithful's consequent lack of access to the Eucharist. He told reporters at the synod that the Sunday after his priestly ordination in 1982, he presided over nine Masses, which is not unusual. That part of his speech was a common theme in dozens of the interventions in the Vatican Synod Hall. But Tagle's call was different: "As we look at the world for threats to the gift of vocation, we should also ask whether the church is a good steward of the gift."[5]

His speech at the 2008 synod on the word of God drew even more attention. The summary of the speech he wrote for publication says, "When people listen to God's word they experience true life. If they refuse, life ends in tragedy. Listening is a serious matter." But it is not something that comes naturally and, especially today, it may even be countercultural, he said.

The church must form hearers of the word. But listening is not transmitted only by teaching but more by a milieu of listening. [He proposed] three approaches for deepening the disposition for listening: 1) Our concern is listening in faith. Faith is a gift of the Spirit, yet it also is an exercise of human freedom. Listening in faith means opening one's heart to God's word, allowing it to penetrate and transform us, and practicing it. It is equivalent to obedience in faith. Formation in listening is integral faith formation. Formation programs should be designed as formation in holistic listening. 2) Events in our world show the tragic effects of the lack of listening: conflicts in families, gaps between generations and nations, and violence. People are trapped in a milieu of monologues, inattentiveness, noise, intolerance, and self-absorption. The church can provide a milieu of dialogue, respect, mutuality, and self-transcendence. 3) God speaks and the church as servant lends its voice to the word. But God does not only speak. God also listens especially to the just, widows, orphans, persecuted, and the poor who have no voice. The church must learn to listen the way God listens and must lend its voice to the voiceless.[6]

He later told Canada's Salt + Light Television that he spent days listening to God in prayer and listening to others before he wrote what was allowed to be only a three-minute speech to the synod. Part of listening, he said, is being attentive and being ready and willing

to be changed, to be transformed, and a readiness to respond. Responding is part of listening. I don't think listening is complete if I have not acted on what I have heard. Listening always involves a mission, always involves conversion, always involves a listening with others because I don't listen as an individual, I listen as a Filipino, I listen as someone who is part of a people with their hopes and their dreams, and my listening adds meaning to the word of God because I believe that God will speak to me; of course, there is the objective word of God in the Scriptures, but that objective word of God comes to me in a unique way and comes to my unique world. I believe that Jesus, who spoke then, continues to speak. He continues to visit the many Marthas and Marys of this world, Jesus continues to visit tombs and cries outside those tombs, Jesus continues to see widows burying their sons and their daughters, Jesus continues to cry with many people, "My God, why have you abandoned me?" We listen to Jesus and we listen to the world around us.[7]

Tagle sealed his reputation as a synod member to pay attention to when as archbishop he addressed the 2012 synod on new evangelization. When other bishops focused on hostility to Christians and Christianity in Western culture, the need to train evangelizers, and the importance of following up initial proclamation of the Gospel with instruction in Catholic doctrine, Tagle talked about humility.

The church must learn humility from Jesus. God's power and might appears in the self-emptying of the Son, in the love that is crucified but truly saves because it is emptied of self for the sake of others. The church is called to follow Jesus' respect for every human person. He defended the dignity of all people, in particular those neglected and despised by the world. Loving his enemies, he affirmed their dignity. The church must discover the power of silence. Confronted with the sorrows, doubts, and uncertainties of people she cannot pretend to give easy solutions. In Jesus, silence becomes the way of attentive listening, compassion, and prayer. It is the way to truth. The seemingly indifferent and aimless societies of our time are earnestly looking for

God. The church's humility, respectfulness, and silence might reveal more clearly the face of God in Jesus. The world takes delight in a simple witness to Jesus—meek and humble of heart.[8]

After having served with Tagle on the general council of the Synod of Bishops, Pope Francis tapped the Filipino cardinal to be one of three presidents of the 2014 extraordinary Synod of Bishops on the family and one of four presidents of the 2015 world synod on the same topic.

The extraordinary synod garnered global news attention for two topics of particular concern in Europe and North America: homosexuality and the pastoral care of divorced and civilly remarried couples. But when the cardinal returned to Manila, he met with the press and insisted the synod was about much more than those two hot-button topics. The purpose of the 2014 gathering, he said, was "simply to surface the different challenges—pastoral challenges—of the family all over the world," setting up a year-long, church-wide reflection about what was said and consulting with others about possible responses so that the 2015 general synod could recommend concrete action. "I think there is wisdom in this," he said, "because in the face of so many complex situations that we find ourselves in today, it is prudent not to rush in order just to have something to say at the end."

He told reporters in Manila, "The synod was aware that there are many signs of hope, not just problems confronting the family. There are many families trying their best, heroically," and many Catholic agencies and movements are supporting families in need. Another important topic, he said, was an apparent decline in faith and an increase in "what Pope Francis called the idolatry of money, the idolatry of success, idolatry of achievement." That led many bishops, especially in Asia and Africa, to call for a deeper investigation into the impact of faith—any religious faith—on relationships and family life, as well as to look at the impact on the family of pressures to work and earn more.

For the Philippines, he said, one big issue is "the monoparent family. There are many different reasons for single parenthood. The traditional idea of a single parent is a single mother, an unmarried woman who has a child. That is true. But in many parts of the world, especially in Asia, single parenthood is not simply a situation of a woman bearing a child out of wedlock. Many single parents have spouses, but they are de facto single parents because of migration. Thus, a man whose wife is working in Hong Kong is a de facto single parent.

"In some parts of the world," he said, "couples separate because they cannot stand each other anymore. But in the Philippines, many married couples separate not because they hate each other. They choose separation because of their love for their family. And they bear the pain of separation just to find jobs elsewhere." The church has a pastoral obligation, he said, to help overseas workers and their families at home so that the couples remain faithful and the family remains strong.

"What distinctly surfaced during the synod," he said, "was the immense variety of cultures, all the more during the sharing of the African and Asian delegates. When I was asked during one press conference to share my experience and observation of the synod, I said I felt I was a student all over again. While my official designation was president-delegate, I did not at all feel like a presider. I felt more like a student, and in fact I took a lot of notes, which I wanted to go back to study more in-depth when I got home."

The cardinal told reporters in the Philippines that despite what they may have seen their colleagues write or broadcast, the synod was not a kind of parliament with blocs of "traditionalists, conservatives, or liberals." It was a gathering of bishops freely and openly sharing their experience and opinions and listening to the experience and opinions of others. "Where there is freedom of expression you will of course expect different views, different opinions," he said. "That is normal for the church. And it is healthy for the church."

Pope Francis encouraged openness and frankness because he "realizes that the world right now is becoming more and more complex. And if we want to address the complex situations we should be at home with diversity and complexity. We should not be shocked by the opinions that are expressed, because in the end, these will serve to enrich the Christian tradition, the word of God, the Bible, the teachings of the church, which have endured through the centuries."

The task of the synod members and the church's leadership, he said, is to ask: "Given the new situations, what do we possess in the great Christian tradition that could help us respond to new situations? So this is not and can never be a betrayal of the Christian faith. In the end we were all motivated by one thing: love of God, love of the church, and love of people who are wounded and in difficult situations. We may have different opinions, but we are united in one love and in love."

The cardinal then told reporters, it is counterproductive and unfair to label others as traditionalists or progressives. "A person will always be deeper than any label. And no person, especially when talking about deep mysteries of love, marriage, relationships, can ever be labeled. It is not helpful to the public. It is not helpful to us and it is not helpful to you to think of human persons based on labels. Let us listen,

listen to the totality, try to understand. And from that understanding we will get a better picture of the event."

When Cardinal Tagle speaks about the importance of listening, there are plenty of Catholics and Catholic pressure groups who see his style as a sign of weakness, as if he is wishy-washy on doctrine. He sees it as being Christian and being Asian. Ministering and evangelizing in a part of the world where Christians have always been a minority, dialogue is a way of life, and the first step in any authentic dialogue is listening.

The Ignatian spirituality in which Cardinal Tagle was molded as a seminarian continues to shape him today. St. Ignatius is very clear about identifying and denouncing evil, but the founder of the Society of Jesus believed it was unhealthy, un-Christian, and unprofitable spiritually to become adept only at identifying evil at the expense of noticing God at work in the world or discerning places where God is calling one to act. Speaking at a conference in Thailand on the New Evangelization sponsored by the Federation of Asian Bishops' Conferences, Cardinal Tagle said, "Without denying the sinfulness, the contradictions, the problems in the contemporary world," the 2012 Synod of Bishops on New Evangelization and *Evangelii Gaudium* remind Catholics that "this world is still God's creation, God is still present in the world, God has not left the world." Jesus was born into this world, he continued, and he died and rose again to save this world. "How come, sometimes, we see the problems clearly, but we are blind to the signs of God's presence, and we are blind to the opportunities, which this broken world offers to us for evangelization?"[9]

Often enough, he said, the opportunities will become obvious only when one is willing to listen to people, especially those who continue to draw joy and hope from their relationship with Jesus even in the midst of the most abject poverty or severe persecution. A Christian—whether a layperson or a cardinal—must nurture humility, the cardinal says frequently. "We are too quick to explain, explain, explain without first listening to the cries. Sometimes the best response is silence, compassionate silence," he said at the Thailand seminar. Two months later, Cardinal Tagle was hosting a kindred spirit in his archdiocese: Pope Francis visited Manila and talked about the grace of compassionate, silent tears when a little girl rescued from the streets asked why such bad things happen to innocent children. The cardinal was in tears, too, as the pope drew the girl to him in a big bear hug.

Indeed, such listening is what Cardinal "Chito" Tagle urges his fellow leaders in the church to practice—a leading by listening. For it is through such passionate service that one models the way of Christ himself.

Notes

Introduction—pages 1–7

1. Luis Antonio G. Tagle, installation homily, Manila Cathedral, quoted at *Priest Stuff* (blog), December 12, 2011, http://prieststuff .blogspot.it/2011/12/archbishop-tagles-homily-on-day-of-his.html.
2. Luis Antonio Tagle, *Telling the Story of Jesus: Word–Communion–Mission* (Collegeville, MN: Liturgical Press, 2015), 58.

Chapter Two:
Vocation—pages 20–31

1. Luis Antonio G. Tagle, "Formation of Priests in the Era of New Evangelization and *Evangelii Gaudium,*" Seminar on Proclaiming the Joy of the Gospel as Renewed Evangelizers in Asia, Federation of Asian Bishops' Conferences Office of Clergy, Pattaya, Thailand, November 10–15, 2014, http://www.fabc.org/offices/oc/Documents /TAGLE%201-Insights%20on%20Clergy%20Formation%20in%20 the%20light%20of%20Synod%20of%20Bishops%20on%20 New%20Evangelization.pdf.

Chapter Three:
Humility and Simplicity—pages 33–45

1. Victor Barreiro Jr., "Tagle's Speech at Ateneo," *Rappler*, March 30, 2013, http://www.rappler.com/move-ph/25125-english-tagle-speech -ateneo/.

2. John L. Allen Jr., "Papabile of the Day: The Men Who Could Be Pope," *National Catholic Reporter*, February 22, 2013, http://ncronline.org/blogs/ncr-today/papabile-day-men-who-could-be-pope-3/.

3. Luis Antonio Tagle, "Concern, Comforting and Reconciling Love for Others," homily at the ordination mass, Manila Cathedral, January 31, 2015, http://www.rcam.org/news/1439-concern-comforting-and-reconciling-love-for-others/.

Chapter Four: On Being a Bishop—pages 46–61

1. Luis Antonio G. Tagle, "Episcopal collegiality in the teaching and practice of Paul VI (1959–1967)" (PhD diss., The Catholic University of America, 1992), later published as *Episcopal Collegiality and Vatican II: The Influence of Paul VI* (Manila: Loyola School of Theology, 2004).

2. Luis Antonio G. Tagle, installation homily, Manila Cathedral, quoted at *Priest Stuff* (blog), December 12, 2011, http://prieststuff.blogspot.it/2011/12/archbishop-tagles-homily-on-day-of-his.html.

Chapter Five: Shaped by Vatican II—pages 62–77

1. Luis Antonio G. Tagle, "Vatican II and Asia's Reception: A Cultural Reading from the Philippines" (speech, Centro Pro Unione, Rome, November 20, 2014); "La Coscienza di una Chiesa Regionale: Inculturazione e Dialogo Interreligioso" (speech, Pontifical Lateran University, Rome, November 21, 2014).

2. Luis Antonio G. Tagle, "The 'Black Week' of Vatican II (November 14–21, 1964)," in *The History of Vatican II*, vol. 4, *Church as Communion: Third Period and Intersession, September 1964–September 1965*, ed. Giuseppe Alberigo and Joseph A. Komonchak (Maryknoll, NY: Orbis, 2003), 449.

3. Ibid., 452.

4. Tagle, "Vatican II and Asia's Reception."

5. International Theological Commission, "*Sensus Fidei* in the Life of the Church" (June 10, 2014), 78, http://www.vatican.va/roman_curia/congregations/cfaith/cti_documents/rc_cti_20140610_sensus-fidei_en.html.

6. Dennis Sadowski, "Cardinal hopes synod will find new ways to share teaching on family," Catholic News Service, May 19, 2014, http://www.catholicnews.com/data/stories/cns/1402050.htm.
7. Luis Antonio G. Tagle, interview with Cindy Wooden for Catholic News Service, October 4, 2014, Rome.
8. Luis Antonio G. Tagle, "The 'Black Week' of Vatican II," 404.

Chapter Six: Lessons of Listening—pages 78–93

1. Luis Antonio Tagle, *Telling the Story of Jesus*, 36.
2. Ibid., 43–45.
3. Ibid., 50–51.
4. Ibid., 25, 31, 32.
5. Tagle, in Holy See Press Office, *Synodus Episcoporum Bulletin*, October 2005, http://www.vatican.va/news_services/press/sinodo/documents/bollettino_21_xi-ordinaria-2005/02_inglese/b12_02.html.
6. Luis Antonio G. Tagle, in Holy See Press Office, *Synodus Episcoporum Bulletin*, October 2008, http://www.vatican.va/news_services/press/sinodo/documents/bollettino_22_xii-ordinaria-2008/xx_plurilingue/b06_xx.html#S.E.R._Mons._Luis_Antonio_G._TAGLE,_Vescovo_di_Imus_(FILIPPINE).
7. Luis Antonio G. Tagle, interview by Thomas Rosica, *Witness*, Salt and Light Television, August 10, 2012, https://www.youtube.com/watch?v=eu4ooS5H8sA.
8. Luis Antonio G. Tagle, in Holy See Press Office, *Synodus Episcoporum Bulletin*, October 2012, http://www.vatican.va/news_services/press/sinodo/documents/bollettino_25_xiii-ordinaria-2012/xx_plurilingue/b07_xx.html#-_S._E._R._Mons._Luis_Antonio_G._TAGLE,_Aricvescovo_di_Manila_(FILIPPINE)_.
9. Luis Antonio G. Tagle, "Formation of Priests in the Era of New Evangelization and *Evangelii Gaudium*," Seminar on Proclaiming the Joy of the Gospel as Renewed Evangelizers in Asia, Federation of Asian Bishops' Conferences Office of Clergy, Pattaya, Thailand, November 10–15, 2014, http://www.fabc.org/offices/oc/Documents/TAGLE%201-Insights%20on%20Clergy%20Formation%20in%20the%20light%20of%20Synod%20of%20Bishops%20on%20New%20Evangelization.pdf.

Bibliography

Primary Sources

Tagle, Luis Antonio. "The 'Black Week' of Vatican II (November 14–21, 1964)." In *History of Vatican II*, vol. 4, *Church as Communion: Third Period and Intersession, September 1964–September 1965*, edited by Giuseppe Alberigo and Joseph A. Komonchak, 387–452. Maryknoll, NY: Orbis, 2003.

———. *Episcopal Collegiality and Vatican II: The Influence of Paul VI*. Manila: Loyola School of Theology, 2004.

———. *Easter People: Living Community*. Maryknoll, NY: Orbis, 2005.

———. *Telling the Story of Jesus: Word–Communion–Mission*. Collegeville, MN: Liturgical Press, 2015.

Interviews

Huang, SJ, Daniel. Interview by Cindy Wooden, December 17, 2014, Curia Generalizia, Rome.

Komonchak, Joseph A. Interview by Cindy Wooden, November 17, 2014, by telephone.

Tagle, Luis Antonio G. Interview with Cindy Wooden, February 15, 2014, Pontificio Collegio Filippino, Rome.

———. Interview with Cindy Wooden, May 12, 2014, Pontificio Collegio Filippino, Rome.

———. Interview with Cindy Wooden, October 4, 2014, Catholic News Service, Rome.

———. Interview with Cindy Wooden, January 11, 2015, Manila.

Index

104